SUPERCONDUCTIVITY: AN ANNOTATED BIBLIOGRAPHY

SUPERCONDUCTIVITY: AN ANNOTATED BIBLIOGRAPHY

EDITED BY
A. BISARSH

Nova Science Publishers, Inc.
Commack, New York

Editorial Production: Susan Boriotti
Office Manager: Annette Hellinger
Graphics: Frank Grucci
Information Editor: Tatiana Shohov
Book Production: Donna Dennis, Patrick Davin, Christine Mathosian, Tammy Sauter and Lynette Van Helden
Circulation: Maryanne Schmidt
Marketing/Sales: Cathy DeGregory

Library of Congress Cataloging-in-Publication Data
available upon request
ISBN 1-56072-106-5

6080 Jericho Turnpike, Suite 207
Commack, New York 11725
Tele. 516-499-3103 Fax 516-499-3146
e-mail: Novascience@earthlink.net
e-mail: Novascil@aol.com
Web Site: http://www.nexusworld.com/nova

Printed in the United States of America

Contents

General

[Gen]Akachi, T. . J.A. Cogordan, and A.A. Valladares.(eds)
Winter Meeting on Low Temperature Physics (10th :
1989 : Cocoyoc, Mexico)
High temperature superconductors : proceedings of
the X Winter Meeting on Low Temperature Physics, Cocoyoc,
Mor., Mexico, 16-18 January 1989,
Singapore ; Teaneck, N.J. : World Scientific, 1989.
QC611.98.H54W56 1989

[Gen]Aksenov, V.L., N.N. Bogolubov, N.M. Plakida
International Seminar on High Temperature
Superconductivity (1989 : Dubna, Chekhovskiæi raæion,
R.S.F.S.R.)
International Seminar on High Temperature
Superconductivity, Dubna, USSR, 28 June-1 July 1989 /
Singapore ; Teaneck, NJ : World Scientific, c1990.
QC611.98.H54I574 1989

[Gen]Andreone, D., R.S. Gonnelli & E. Mezzetti.
Advances in high temperature superconductivity :
Torino, Italy, 18-20 November 1991 / edited by I.S.I., D.
Andreone, R.S. Gonnelli & E. Mezzetti.
Singapore ; River Edge, NJ : World Scientific, c1992.
QC611.98.H54A39 1992

[Gen]Asimov, Isaac, 1920-
How did we find out about superconductivity? /
Isaac Asimov ; illustrated by Erika Kors.
New York : Walker, 1988.
QC612.S8A75 1988

[Gen]Bando, Y. , H. Yamauchi, (eds.)
International Symposium on Superconductivity (5th
1992 : K¯obe-shi, Japan)
Advances in superconductivity V : proceedings of
the 5th International Symposium on Superconductivity (ISS
'92), November 16-19, 1992, Kobe /

Berlin ; New York : Springer-Verlag, c1993.
QC611.9.I57 1992

[Gen]Baquero, R.(ed.).
CINVESTAV Superconductivity Symposium (1st : 1990
Oaxtepec, Mexico)
Electron-phonon interaction in oxide
superconductors : proceedings of the First CINVESTAV
Superconductivity Symposium, Oaxtepec, Mexico, 11-14
December, 1990
Singapore ; River Edge, N.J. : World Scientific, c1991.
QC611.98.C64C56 1990

[Gen]Baran, M. W. Gorzkowski, H. Szymczak
International Workshop on Critical Current
Limitations in High Temperature Superconductors (1991 :
Zaborów, Poland)
Proceedings of the International Workshop on
Critical Current Limitations in High Temperature
Superconductors, Zaborów near Warsaw, Poland, September
10-13, 1991.
Singapore ; River Edge, NJ : World Scientific, c1992.
QC611.98.H54I585 1991

[Gen]Barone,Antonio and Anatoli Larkin
Soviet-Italian Symposium on Weak
Superconductivity (2nd : 1987 : Naples, Italy)
Proceedings of the 2nd Soviet-Italian Symposium
on Weak Superconductivity : May 1987, Naples, Italy /
; organized by the Consiglio nazionale delle ricerche of Italy, the Academy of Sciences of
USSR, the Istituto italiano per gli studi filosofici.
Singapore ; Teaneck, NJ, USA : World Scientific, c1987.
QC612.S8S68 1987

[Gen]Baskaran, G.
Adriatico Research Conference and Miniworkshop on
Strongly Correlated Electron Systems II (1990 : Trieste, Italy)
Strongly correlated electron systems II :
proceedings of the Adriatico research conference and
miniworkshop, ICTP, Trieste, Italy, 18 June-27 July 1990 /
Singapore ; Teaneck, NJ : World Scientific, c1991.
QC176.8.E4S794 1991

[Gen]Bedell, Kevin (ed.)

High temperature superconductivity : the Los
Alamos symposium--1989 : proceedings
Redwood City, Calif. : Addison-Wesley Pub. Co.,
Advanced Book Program, c1990.
QC611.98.H54H54345 1990

[Gen]Bednorz, J.G. K.A. Müller, (eds)
Earlier and recent aspects of superconductivity :
lectures from the international school, Erice, Trapani,
Sicily, July 4-16, 1989 /.
Berlin ; New York : Springer-Verlag, c1990.
QC611.9.E27 1990

[Gen]Beyermann,W.P. N.L.Huang-Liu, D.E. MacLaughlin.
Raymond L. Orbach Inauguration Symposium (1993 :
University of California, Riverside)
Random magnetism, high temperature
superconductivity : proceedings of the Raymond L. Orbach
Inauguration Symposium, University of California at
Riverside, March 19-20, 1993 /
Singapore ; River Edge, N.J. : World Scientific, c1994.
QC176.8.S68R39 1993

[Gen]Billings, Charlene W.
Superconductivity : from discovery to
breakthrough / Charlene W. Billings.
New York : Cobblehill Books/Dutton, c1991.
QC611.922.B55 1991

[Gen]Block, Martin M.
Aspen Winter Physics Conference (1st : 1985)
First Aspen Winter Physics Conference / edited by
Martin M. Block.
New York, N.Y. : New York Academy of Sciences, 1986.
Q11.N5 vol. 461; Alternative class.: QC793

[Gen]Burnham, Calvin G.(ed.)
World Congress on Superconductivity (2nd : 1990 :
Houston, Tex.)
2nd World Congress on Superconductivity, Houston,
Texas, 10-13 September 1990 / editor,
Singapore ; River Edge, N.J. : World Scientific, 1992.
QC611.9.W68 1990

[Gen]Burns, Gerald, 1932-
High-temperature superconductivity : an
introduction / Gerald Burns.
Boston : Academic Press, c1992.
QC611.98.H54B87 1992

[Gen]Butcher, P.N. (ed.)
ICTP Spring College in Condensed Matter on
"Superconductivity" (1992 : Trieste, Italy)
Superconductivity : from basic physics to the
latest developments : International Centre for
Physics, Trieste, Italy, April 27-June 19, 1992
notes of the ICTP Spring College in Condensed
"Superconductivity" /
Singapore ; River Edge, N.J. : World Scientific, c1995.
QC611.92.I28 1992

[Gen]Cabrera, Blas, H.Gutfreund, and Vladimir Kresin.
From high-temperature superconductivity to
microminiature refrigeration /
New York : Plenum Press, c1996.
QC611.98.H54F76 1996

[Gen]California. Legislature. Joint Committee on
Science and Technology.
Governor's proposals on collaborative research &
superconductivity : hearing, State of California, State
Capitol, Room 2040, Sacramento, California, Wednesday, June
15, 1988 / Joint Committee on Science and Technology and
Assembly Committee on Economic Development and New
Technologies ; reported by Evelyn Mizak.
Sacramento, CA : Joint Committee on Science and
Technology : Additional copies may be purchased from Joint
Publications, [1988]
KFC10.S35 1988c

[Gen]Chiofalo, M. L. G. Iadonisi, and R. J. Schrieffer,, eds
Models and phenomenology for conventional and
high-temperature superconductivity /
Burke, VA : IOS Press, 1998.
9811 BOOK NOT YET IN LC

[Gen]CINVESTAV Superconductivity Symposium (2nd : 1992
: Tequisquiapán, Mexico)

Manifestations of the electron-phonon interaction
: proceedings of the 2nd CINVESTAV Superconductivity
Symposium, Tequisquiapan, Mexico, 2-6 November 1992 / editor,
Rafael Baquero.
Singapore ; River Edge, NJ : World Scientific, c1994.
QC793.5.E628C56 1992

[Gen]Czechoslovak-Italian Symposium on
Superconductivity (2nd : 1991 : Smolenice, Slovakia)
Proceedings of 2nd Czechoslovak-Italian Symposium
on Superconductivity : Smolenice, CSFR, 14-16 May 1991.
[S.l. : s.n., 1991?] (Bratislava : Ofprint J. Holik)
QC611.9.C94 1991

[Gen]Dahl, Per F., 1932-
Superconductivity : its historical roots and
development from mercury to the ceramic oxides / Per Fridtjof Dahl.
New York : American Institute of Physics, c1992.
QC611.92.D34 1992

[Gen]Davydov, A.S. , V.M. Loktev, eds.
High-Tõc superconductivity : experiment and
theory / Berlin ; New York : Springer-Verlag, c1992.
QC611.98.H54H49 1992

[Gen]Deaver, B,. and John Ruvalds(eds.)
NATO Advanced Study Institute on Advances in
Superconductivity (1982 : Erice, Italy)
Advances in superconductivity
New York : Plenum Press, c1983.
QC612.S8N367 1982

[Gen]Delic, George, Mary F.Wheeler
Next generation environmental models and
computational methods / edited by George Delic, Mary F. Wheeler.
Philadelphia : Society for Industrial and Applied
Mathematics, c1997.
GE45.D37N49 1997

[Gen]DeWeese, Mary E.
High-temperature superconductivity : abstracts of
NIST publications, 1987-1991 / edited by Mary E. DeWeese.
Gaithersburg, MD : U.S. Dept. of Commerce,
National Institute of Standards and Technology, 1991.

[Gen]Dew-Hughes, D.(ed.).
European Conference on Applied Superconductivity
(2nd : 1995 : Edinburgh, Scotland)
Applied superconductivity 1995 : proceedings of
EUCAS 1995, the second European Conference on Applied
Superconductivity, held in Edinburgh, Scotland, 3-6 July 1995
Bristol ; Philadelphia : Institute of Physics. Pub., 1995.
TK7872.S8E87 1995

[Gen]Doss, James D.
Engineer's guide to high-temperature
superconductivity / James D. Doss.
New York : Wiley, c1989.
QC611.98.H54D67 1989

[Gen]Douglass, D. Jr.,and R. W. Schmitt, assisted by G. E. Nichols.
International Conference on the Science of
Superconductivity, Colgate University, 1963.
International Conference on the Science of
Superconductivity; [proceedings. Edited by
New York? 1964]
QC612.S8I5 1963

[Gen]Evetts, J.(ed.)
High temperature superconductivity : proceedings
of LT-19 Satellite Conference, Cambridge, 13-15 August 1990 /
Bristol, England ; Philadelphia : A. Hilger, c1991.
QC611.98.H54H54358 1991

[Gen]Ferdighini, Carlo and Antonio S. Siri (eds)
High temperature superconductivity : proceedings
of the Third National Meeting, 12-14 February 1990, Genova,
Italy Singapore ; Teaneck, NJ : World Scientific, 1990.
QC611.98.H54H543452 1990

[Gen]Firth, I. M. (Ian Mason)
Superconductivity [by] I. M. Firth.
London, Mills and Boon, 1972.
QC612.S8F48 1972

[Gen]Fishlock, David.
A guide to superconductivity, edited by David Fishlock.
London, Macdonald; New York, American Elsevier [1969]
QC612.S8F5

[Gen]Fujita, T., and Y. Shiohara, eds.
Advances in superconductivity VI : proceedings of
the 6th International Symposium on Superconductivity (ISS
'93), October 26-29, 1993, Hiroshima /
Tokyo ; New York : Springer-Verlag, c1994.
QC611.9.A38 1994

[Gen]Gan, Z.Z., S.S. Xie & Z.X. Zhao.
High-temperature superconductivity (BHTSC '92) :
proceedings of the Beijing international conference /
Singapore ; River Edge, N.J. : World Scientific, c1993.
QC611.98.H54H5434516 1993

[Gen]Garg, K.B. and D.C. Jain (eds)
International Symposium on High Temperature
Superconductivity (1988 : Dept. of Physics, University of Rajasthan)
Proceedings of the International Symposium on
High Temperature Superconductivity, 6-8 July 1988, Department
of Physics, University of Rajasthan, Jaipur, India /
New Delhi : Oxford & IBH Pub. Co., c1989.
QC611.98.H54I575 1988

[Gen]Georg Bednorz: exploring superconductivity / IMG
Educators with the assistance of the Nobel Foundation.
United States : Sunburst Communications, Inc., 1990.
VAB 3514 (viewing copy)

[Gen]Ginzburg, V. L. (Vitaliæi Lazarevich), 1916-
Superconductivity / V.L. Ginzburg, E.A. Andryushin.
Singapore ; River Edge, NJ : World Scientific, c1994.
QC611.92.G56 1994

[Gen]Gregory, W. D. , W. N. Mathews, Jr., and E. A. Edelsack. (ed.)
The Science and technology of superconductivity.
New York, Plenum Press, 1973.
TK7872.S8S34

[Gen]Gupta, L.C. and M.S. Multani (eds)
Selected topics in superconductivity
Singapore ; River Edge, NJ : World Scientific, c1993.
QC611.92.S45 1993
[Gen]Hayakawa, H. and N. Koshizuka, (eds.)
International Symposium on Superconductivity (4th
: 1991 : Tokyo, Japan)

Advances in superconductivity IV : proceedings of
the 4th International Symposium on Superconductivity (ISS
'91), October 14-17, 1991, Tokyo
Tokyo ; New York : Springer-Verlag, c1992.
QC611.98.C64I57 1991

[Gen]Hazen, Robert M., 1948-
The breakthrough : the race for the
superconductor / Robert M. Hazen.
New York : Summit Books, c1988.
QC611.96.H39 1988

[Gen]High temperature superconductivity in perspective.
Washington, DC : Congress of the U.S., Office of
Technology Assessment : For sale by the Supt. of Docs., U.S.
G.P.O., [1990]
QC611.98.H54H54343 1990

[Gen]High-temperature superconductivity : reprints
from Physical review letters and Physical review B :
January-June 1987.
Woodbury, N.Y. : Published by the American
Physical Society through the American Institute of Physics, c1987-
QC612.S8H54 1987

[Gen]Hunt, V. Daniel.
Superconductivity sourcebook / V. Daniel Hunt.
New York : Wiley, c1989.
QC611.92.H86 1989

[Gen]International Symposium on Superconductivity.
Advances in superconductivity : proceedings of
the ... International Symposium on Superconductivity.
Tokyo ; New York : Springer-Verlag,
QC611.9.I56a

[Gen]International Symposium on Weak Superconductivity
(7th : 1994 : Bratislava, Solvak)
Proceedings of the Seventh International
Symposium on Weak Superconductivity, June 6-10, 1994,
Smolenice Castle, Slovak Republic / editors, ^S. Be^na^cka,
P. Seidel and V. ^Strbâ¸k.
Bratislava, Slovak Republic : Dept. of
Cryoelectronics, Institute of Electrical Engineering, c1994.

[Gen]Ishiguro, T. K. Kajimura (eds.)
International Symposium on Superconductivity (2nd 1989 : Tsukuba Kenky¯u Gakuen Toshi, Japan)
Advances in superconductivity II : proceedings of the 2nd International Symposium on Superconductivity (ISS '89) November 14-17, 1989, Tsukuba ; ISTEC.
Tokyo ; New York : Springer-Verlag, c1990.
QC611.9.I57 1989

[Gen]Journal of superconductivity.
New York : Plenum Press, c1988-
QC611.9.J68

[Gen]Kajimura, K. and H. Hayakawa (eds.).
International Symposium on Superconductivity (3rd : 1990 : Sendai-shi, Miyagi-ken, Japan)
Advances in superconductivity III: proceedings of the 3rd International Symposium on Superconductivity (ISS '90), November 6-9, 1990, Sendai /
Tokyo ; New York : Springer-Verlag, c1991.
QC611.9.I57 1990

[Gen]Kamimura, H. , A. Oshiyama (eds.).
NEC Symposium (2nd : 1988 : Hakone-machi, Japan)
Mechanisms of high temperature superconductivity : proceedings of the 2nd NEC Symposium, Hakone, Japan, October 24-27, 1988
Berlin ; New York : Springer-Verlag, c1989.
QC611.98.H54N43 1988

[Gen]Ketterson, J. B. (John Boyd)
Superconductivity / J.B. Ketterson and S.N. Song.
New York : Cambridge University Press, 1998.
QC611.95.K48 1998

[Gen]Kitazawa, K. T. Ishiguro,(eds.)
International Symposium on Superconductivity (1st : 1988 : Nagoya-shi, Japan)
Advances in superconductivity : proceedings of the 1st International Symposium on Superconductivity (ISS '88), August 28-31, 1988, Nagoya
Tokyo ; New York : Springer-Verlag, c1989.
QC611.94.I57 1988

[Gen]Klamut, J.(ed.)
Recent developments in high temperature superconductivity : proceedings of the 1st Polish-US conference, held at Wroclaw and Duszniki Zdrój, Poland, 11-15 September 1995 / Berlin ; New York : Springer, c1996.
QC611.98.H54R43 1996

[Gen]Kojima, Y.(ed.).
Workshop on RF-Superconductivity (4th : 1989 : Tsukuba-shi, Japan)
Proceedings of the 4th Workshop on RF Superconductivity, August 14-18, 1989, KEK, Tsukuba, Japan / Tsukuba-shi, Ibaraki-ken, Japan : National Laboratory for High Energy Physics, c1990.
QC611.9.W67 1989

[Gen]Kresin, Vladimir Z.
Fundamentals of superconductivity / Vladimir Z. Kresin and Stuart A. Wolf.
New York : Plenum Press, c1990.
QC611.92.K74 1990

[Gen]Kresin, Vladimir Z.
Mechanisms of conventional and high Tc superconductivity / Vladimir Z. Kresin, Hans Morawitz, Stuart A. Wolf.
New York : Oxford University Press, 1993.
QC611.92.K75 1993

[Gen]Langone, John, 1929-
Superconductivity : the new alchemy / John Langone.
Chicago : Contemporary Books, c1989.
TK7872.S8L36 1989

[Gen]Larkin, A.I., and N.V. Zavaritsky
High temperature superconductivity for Russia /
Singapore ; Teaneck, N.J. : World Scientific, c1989.
QC611.98.H54H5434 1989

[Gen]Lundqvist , S. et al.
Adriatico Research Conference on High Temperature Superconductors (1987 : Trieste, Italy)
Proceedings of the Adriatico Research Conference on High Temperature Superconductors, ICTP, Trieste, Italy,

5-8 July 1987
Singapore ; Teaneck, NJ, USA : World Scientific, c1987.
QC611.98.H54A37 1987

[Gen]Lynton, E. A. (Ernest Albert)
Superconductivity [by] E. A. Lynton.
London, Methuen, 1969.
QC612.S8L9 1969

[Gen]Maekawa, S. M. Sato, eds.
Toshiba International School of Superconductivity
(1991 : Kyoto, Japan)
Physics of high-temperature superconductors :
proceedings of the Toshiba International School of
Superconductivity (ITS_p2_s), Kyoto, Japan, July 15-20, 1991
Berlin ; New York : Springer-Verlag, c1992.
QC611.98.H54T67 1991

[Gen]Masuda, Kohzoh et al.
Tsukuba Seminar on High Tc Superconductivity
(1989 : Tsukuba-shi, Japan)
Proceedings of the Tsukuba Seminar on High Tc
Superconductivity : Tsukuba, Japan, May 31-June 2, 1989 /
Tsukuba : University of Tsukuba, [1989]
QC611.98.H54T78 1989

[Gen]Menash, Thomas O.
Superconductor engineering / Thomas O. Menash, editor.
New York, N.Y. : American Institute of Chemical
Engineers, 1992.
QC611.97.C54S86 1992

[Gen]Metzger , Robert M.
High temperature superconductivity : the first
two years : proceedings of a conference held 11-13 April
1988, Tuscaloosa, Alabama.
New York : Gordon and Breach Science Publishers, c1989.
QC611.98.H54H544 1989

[Gen]Miller, Richard K., and Matthew Walker, editors.
Superconductivity update /
Lilburn, Ga. : The Fairmont Press, 1989.
[Gen]Muller, Jean, 1929-
Phenomenological aspects of superconductivity.

Lectures given in the Academic training programme of Cern, 1967-1968.
Geneva, CERN, 1969.
QC770.E82 1969, no. 9

[Gen]National Research Program 30 High Temperature Superconductivity.
National Research Program 30 High Temperature Superconductivity : final report.
Bern : Schweizerischer Nationalfonds zur Förderung der wissenschaftlichen Forschung, Abt. Nationale Forschungsprogramme und Schwerpunktprogramme, [199-]
IN PROCESS

[Gen]Nicolsky , Roberto et al.
Latin-American Conference on High Temperature Superconductivity (1st : 1988 : Rio de Janeiro, Brazil)
First Latin-American Conference on High Temperature Superconductivity, 4-6 May 1988, Rio de Janeiro, Brazil : proceedings of the I LACHTS /
Singapore ; New Jersey : World Scientific, 1988.
QC611.98.H54L38 1988

[Gen]Nowotny, Helga.
After the breakthrough : the emergence of high-temperature superconductivity as a research field /
Helga Nowotny, Ulrike Felt.
Cambridge ; New York : Cambridge University Press, 1997.
QC611.98.H54N69 1997

[Gen]Olzi, E. and S. Zannella.(eds.)
National Congress on High Tc Superconductivity (8th : 1996 : Como, Italy)
Proceedings of the 8th National Congress on High Temperature Superconductivity : Como, October 1-4, 1996 /
[Bologna : Società italiana di fisica, c1997]
QC611.98.H54N33 1996

[Gen]Ott, H.R. (ed.)
Ten years of superconductivity, 1980-1990 /
edited by H.R. Ott.
Dordrecht ; Boston : Kluwer Academic, c1993.
QC611.92.T46 1993

[Gen]Pachauri, R.K., and Sanjeev Mukerjee (eds)
High temperature superconductivity : promise and
prospects,
New Delhi : Tata Energy Research Institute, c1989.
QC611.98.H54H543453 1989

[Gen]Palmer, D.N.(ed.)
Superconductivity advances and applications, 1989
presented at the Winter Annual Meeting of the American
Society of Mechanical Engineers, San Francisco, California,
December 10-15, 1989 / sponsored by the Superconductivity
Technical Committee of the Advanced Energy Systems Division,
ASME ;.
New York, N.Y. : ASME, c1989.
QP82.2.M3S86 1989

[Gen]Physica B + C [microform].
Amsterdam : North-Holland Pub. Co., 1975-1988.
Microfilm 90/6956

[Gen]Physica B + C.
Amsterdam : North-Holland Pub. Co., 1975-1988.
QC1.P3833

[Gen]Physica. C, Superconductivity [microform].
Amsterdam : North-Holland, 1988-
Microfilm (o) 91/6008

[Gen]Physica. C, Superconductivity.
Amsterdam : North-Holland, 1988-
QC611.9.P49

[Gen]Plakida, N. M. (Nikolaæi Maksimilianovich)
Uniform Title: Vysokotemperaturnye sverkhprovodniki. English
High-temperature superconductivity : experiment
and theory / Nikolai M. Plakida.
Berlin ; New York : Springer, c1995.
QC611.98.H54P5313 1995

[Gen]Poole, Charles P.
Handbook of superconductivity / Charles P.Poole.
San Diego, CA : Academic Press, 1999.

[Gen]Poole, Charles P.
Superconductivity / Charles P. Poole, Jr.,
Horacio A. Farach, Richard J. Creswick.
San Diego : Academic Press, c1995.
QC611.92.P66 1995

[Gen]Projects on "High temperature superconductivity"
Azerbaijan, Armenia, Estonia, Byelorussia, Russia,
Ukraine.
Moscow : International Centre for Scientific and
Technical Information, 1992.
QC611.98.H54P77 1992

[Gen]Rose-Innes, Alistair Christopher.
Introduction to superconductivity / by A. C.
Rose-Innes and E. H. Rhoderick.
Oxford ; New York : Pergamon Press, c1969, 1976 printing.
QC612.S8R6 1976

[Gen]Rose-Innes, Alistair Christopher.
Introduction to superconductivity / by A. C.
Rose-Innes and E. H. Rhoderick.
Oxford ; New York : Pergamon Press, 1978.
QC612.S8R6 1978

[Gen]Rose-Innes, Alistair Christopher.
Introduction to superconductivity, by A. C.
Rose-Innes and E. H. Rhoderick.
Oxford, New York, Pergamon Press [1969]
QC612.S8R6 1969

[Gen]Salama,(K.) C.W. Chu, W.K. Chu. (eds.)
US-Japan Workshop on High Tc Superconductors (6th
1993: University of Houston)
Proceedings of the Sixth US-Japan Workshop on
High Tōc Superconductors, Texas Center for Superconductivity,
University of Houston, Houston, Texas, U.S.A., December 6-7,
1993 Singapore ; River Edge, N.J. : World Scientific, c1994.
QC611.98.H54U8 1993

[Gen]SciCentral
Address: http://scicentral.com/P-superc.html
Superconductivity Comprehensive Directories ; Specialized Resources ; Databases;
Selected Articles ; Superconductivity Links; Superconductivity Papers Database NIST

High Temperature Superconducting Materials Databases .

[Gen]Science research abstracts journal. Part A: Superconductivity, magnetohydrodynamics and plasmas, theoretical physics.
Riverdale, Md., Cambridge Scientific Abstracts.

[Gen]Science research abstracts journal. Part B: Laser and electro-optic reviews, quantum electronics and unconventional energy sources.
Riverdale, Md. : Cambridge Scientific Abstracts,

[Gen]Series on progress in high temperature superconductivity.
Singapore ; Teaneck, N.J., USA : World Scientific, c1987-

[Gen]Sheahen, Thomas P.
Introduction to high-temperature superconductivity / Thomas P. Sheahen.
New York : Plenum Press, c1994.
QC611.98.H54S48 1994

[Gen]Solid state abstracts journal.
Cambridge, Mass. : Cambridge Communications Corp., c1967-c1987.
TK7800.S6

[Gen]Solid state and superconductivity abstracts.
Bethesda, MD : Cambridge Scientific Abstracts, c1988-
TK7800.S6

[Gen]Superconductivity bulletin : progress in HTS electric power applications / Department of Energy, Conservation and Renewable Energy, office of Utility Technologies.
[Argonne, Ill. : Argonne National Laboratory,

[Gen]Superconductivity Meetings and Conferences
http://www.sucon.cam.ac.uk/links/confs.html

[Gen]Superconductivity review.
Philadelphia : Gordon and Breach Science Publishers, 1992-

QC611.9.S856

[Gen]Superconductor industry.
[Ramsey, N.J. : Rodman Pub. Corp., 1988-
NOT IN LC

[Gen]Superconductor news.
[El Toro, CA : Superconductor Applications
Association,

[Gen]Superconductor science & technology (Online)
Superconductor science & technology [computer file].
[London?]: IOP Pub., 1966-
QC612.S8S964
Access:

[Gen]Superconductor week.
Washington, D.C. : Atlantic Information Services,

[Gen]Superconductors / project directors, William P.
Weizer, Martin Hersch.
Cleveland Heights, Ohio : Freedonia Group, c1987.
HD9696.S963U67 1987

[Gen]Sverkhprovodimost'. English.
Superconductivity.
New York, N.Y. : American Institute of Physics,
QC611.9.S885

[Gen]Sznajd, Józef.
III National Symposium on High-Tc
Superconductivity, Wroclaw 91 : (October 21st & 22nd, 1991) :
abstracts / edited by Józef Sznajd, Maciej Kazimierski.
Wroclaw : Instytut Niskich Temperatur i Badaân
Strukturalnych. PAN, 1991.

[Gen]Taubes, Gary.
Nobel dreams : power, deceit, and the ultimate
experiment / Gary Taubes.
New York : Random House, c1986.
QC793.4.T38 1986

[Gen]Taylor, A. W. B.
Superconductivity [by] A.W.B. Taylor.
London, Wykeham, 1970.
QC612.S8T39

[Gen]The superconductivity industry : opportunities /
prepared in cooperation with Advanced Technologies
Enterprises, Inc.
Stamford, Conn. : Business Communications Co., [1997?]
HD9696.S962S86 1997

[Gen]Tinkham, Michael.
Introduction to superconductivity / Michael Tinkham.
New York : McGraw-Hill, [1975]
QC612.S8T49

[Gen]Tinkham, Michael.
Introduction to superconductivity / Michael Tinkham.
Huntington, N.Y. : R. E. Krieger Pub. Co., 1980, c1975.
QC612.S8T49 1980

[Gen]Tinkham, Michael.
Introduction to superconductivity / Michael Tinkham.
New York : McGraw Hill, c1996.
QC611.92.T56 1996

[Gen]Tournier, R. and R. Suryanarayanan
ICMAS 90 (1990)
ICMAS 90, from modern superconductivity towards
applications : proceedings of the international conference /
; sponsored
by IITT-International.
Gournay-sur-Marne : IITT-International, [1992?]
TK7872.S8I26 1990

[Gen]Tunstall, D.P. and W. Barford.
Scottish Universities' Summer School in Physics
(39th : 1991 : St. Andrews, Scotland)
High temperature superconductivity : proceedings
of the thirty-ninth Scottish Universities Summer School in
Physics, St. Andrews, June 1991
Bristol ; Philadelphia : Scottish Universities
Summer School in Physics & Adam Hilger, c1991.
QC611.98.H54S26 1991

[Gen]United States. Congress. House. Committee on
Science, Space, and Technology.
Superconductivity : hearing before the Committee
on Science, Space, and Technology, House of Representatives,

One hundredth Congress, first session, June 10, 1987.
Washington : U.S. G.P.O. : For sale by Supt. of
Docs., Congressional Sales Office, U.S. G.P.O., 1988.
KF27.S39 1987f

[Gen]United States. Congress. House. Committee on
Science, Space, and Technology. Subcommittee on Energy
Research and Development.
High-temperature superconductivity technology
transfer : hearing before the Subcommittee on Energy Research
and Development of the Committee on Science, Space, and
Technology, House of Representatives, One Hundredth Congress,
second session, June 23, 1988.
Washington : U.S. G.P.O. : For sale by the Supt.
of Docs., Congressional Sales Office, U.S. G.P.O., 1988.
KF27.S3935 1988

[Gen]United States. Congress. House. Committee on
Science, Space, and Technology. Subcommittee on
Transportation, Aviation, and Materials.
Superconductivity : hearing before the
Subcommittee on Transportation, Aviation, and Materials of
the Committee on Science, Space, and Technology, U.S. House
of Representatives, One Hundred First Congress, first
session, October 31, 1989.
Washington : U.S. G.P.O. : For sale by the Supt.
of Docs., Congressional Sales Office, U.S. G.P.O., 1990.
KF27.S3997 1989m

[Gen]United States. Congress. House. Committee on
Science, Space, and Technology. Subcommittee on
Transportation, Aviation, and Materials.
Superconductivity : hearing before the
Subcommittee on Transportation, Aviation, and Materials of
the Committee on Science, Space, and Technology,
U.S. House of Representatives,
One Hundred First Congress, second session, February 21, 1990.
Washington : U.S. G.P.O. : For sale by the Supt.
of Docs., Congressional Sales Office, U.S. G.P.O., 1990.
KF27.S3997 1990f

[Gen]United States. Congress. Senate. Committee on
Governmental Affairs.
U.S. efforts to commercialize superconductivity :

hearing before the Committee on Governmental Affairs, United
States Senate, One Hundredth Congress, second session, June 28, 1988.
Washington : U.S. G.P.O. : For sale by the Supt.
of Docs., Congressional Sales Office, U.S. G.P.O., 1989.
KF26.G67 1988n

[Gen]United States. National Commission on Superconductivity.
Report of the National Commission on Superconductivity.
[Washington, DC] : The Commission, [1990]
TK7872.S8U55 1990

[Gen]Vanston, John H. et al.
Superconductivity : a practical guide for decision makers
Austin, Tex. (6034 W. Courtyard Dr., Suite 380,
Austin 78730) : Technology Futures, c1988.
QC611.98.H54S87 1988

[Gen]Vidali, Gianfranco.
Superconductivity : the next revolution? /Gianfranco Vidali.
Cambridge [England] ; New York, NY, USA :
Cambridge University Press, 1993.
QC611.92.V53 1993

[Gen]Wallace , P. R.
Advanced Summer Study Institute on
Superconductivity (1st : 1968 : McGill University)
Superconductivity; proceedings.
New York, Gordon and Breach [1969]
QC612.S8A38 1968

[Gen]Wu, P.T.(ed.)
Taiwan International Symposium on
Superconductivity (2nd : 1989 : Hsin-chu-shih (Taiwan)
Superconductivity and applications : proceedings
of the Taiwan International Symposium on Superconductivity,
17-19 April, 1989, Hsinchu, Taiwan.
Singapore ; New Jersey : World Scientific, c1989.
QC611.98.H54T35 1989

[Gen]Zhou, Shu-Ang.
Electrodynamics of solids and microwave
superconductivity / Shu-Ang Zhou.
New York : John Wiley, 1999.
QC631.Z565 1999

Theory

[A]A.V. Narlikar (Ed.)
Studies of High Temperature Superconductors. Volume 1
1989. 382 pages, $145. ISBN 0-941743-54-3.
Superconductivity; Physics, Chemistry, Materials Science, Solid State Electronics, Engineeering
Contents: Oxygen Hole Mechanism of Superconductivity in Cuprates and other Metal Oxides (C.N.R. Rao - Indian Inst. of Science, Bangalore, India); Electronically Driven Instabilities in High Tc Superconductors and Related Materials; The BCS Pairing and Possible Mechanisms for High Tc Superconductivity; Boson Exchange Mechanisms, Bounds and Asymtotic Limits; A Strong Coupling Approach to High Temperature Superconductors; Ion Beam Modification and Analysis of Thin $YBa_2Cu_3O_7$ Films; Superconducting Properties Associated with Short Coherence Length - Fluctuation Effect and Flux Creep Phenomenon in HTSC; Basic Thin Film Processing for High Tc Superconductors; Three Terminal High Tc Superconducting Devices with Large Current Gain; Twins in High Tc $YBa_2Cu_3O_{7-\_}$ Superconductors; The Role of Mott-Insulation, Non-Stoichiometry and Altered Valence in High Tc Superconductivity; Sound Velocity and Elastic Constants in Oxide Superconductors; X-Ray Photoelectron Spectroscopic Studies of High Tc Oxide Superconductors; Synthesis of High Tc Oxide Superconductors in Y-, Bi- and Tl- Systems: The Role of Chemistry; Substitutional Studies on High Temperature Superconductors.

[A]Accetta, Frank S.
Phase transitions in bosonic superconducting strings [microform]/ by Frank S. Accetta.
1988.
Microfilm 91/78 (Q)

[A]Akutsu, Hiroki; Arai, Emiko; Kobayashi, Hayao; Highly correlated organic conductor with magnetic anions exhibiting a p-d coupled metal-insulator transition, l-(BETS)2FeBrxCl4-x(BETS = bis(ethylenedithio)tetraselenafulvalene); Journal of the American Chemical Society.v. 119 Dec. 24 '97 p. 12681-2.
The conducting properties of l-(BETS)2FeCl4 (BETS = bis(ethylenedithio)tetraselenafulvalene) were studied. This organic conductor displayed an unexpectedly large metal-insulator transition temperature increase and a contrastive strong Fe Fe antiferromagnetic interaction decrease upon partial exchange of the Cl with Br. This observation suggests a novel "spin structure model" characteristic of highly correlated organic conducting systems with magnetic anions and highlights the

importance of p-d coupling.

[A]Al'tov, V.A.
Stabilizaëtisiëiia sverkhprovodëiiashchikh
magnitnykh sistem / V.A. Al'tov ... [et al.]; pod
redakëtisieæi V.V. Sycheva.
Moskva : çEnergoatomizdat, 1984.
QC761.3.S7 1984

[A]Allen M. Goldman and Stuart A. Wolf. (eds.)
NATO Advanced Study Institute on Percolation,
Localization, and Superconductivity (1983 : Savoie, France)
Percolation, Localization, and superconductivity
/ edited by Allen M. Goldman and Stuart A. Wolf.
New York : Plenum Press, published in cooperation
with NATO Scientific Affairs Division, c1984.
QC176.A1N326 1983

[A]Anderson, P. W. (Philip W.), 1923-
The theory of superconductivity in the high-Tc
cuprates / P.W. Anderson.
Princeton, N.J. : Princeton University Press, c1997.
QC611.98.C64A54 1997

[A]Anderson, Philip W.; c-axis electrodynamics as evidence for the interlayer theory of high-temperature superconductivity; Science.v. 279 no5354 Feb. 20 '98 p. 1196-8.
In the interlayer theory of high-temperature superconductivity, the interlayer pair tunneling energy (similar to the Josephson or Lawrence-Doniach energy) is the motivation for superconductivity. This connection requires two experimentally verifiable identities: the coherent normal-state conductance must be smaller than the "Josephson" coupling energy, and the Josephson coupling energy must be equal to the condensation energy of the superconductor. The first condition is well satisfied in the only case that is relevant, (La,Sr)2CuO4, but the second condition has been questioned.

[A]Anderson, Philip W.; When the electron falls apart; Physics Today.v. 50 Oct. '97 p. 42-7.
Part of a special section on electrons.

[A]Aronov,, A.A. A.I. Larkin, and V.S. Lutovinov.
International Conference on High Temperature
Superconductivity and Localization Phenomena (1991 : Moscow,
R.S.F.S.R.)
Proceedings of the International Conference on
High Temperature Superconductivity and Localization

Phenomena, Moscow, USSR, 11-17 May 1991 / editors,
Singapore ; River Edge, N.J. : World Scientific, c1992.
QC611.98.H54I55 1991

[A]Ashkenazi, Josef
High-temperature superconductivity : physical
properties, microscopic theory, and mechanisms
New York : Plenum Press, c1991.
QC611.98.H54H543453 1992

[A]Ausloos, Marcel and Andrei A.Varlamov.
Fluctuation phenomena in high temperature
superconductors / edited by Marcel Ausloos and Andrei A.
Varlamov.
Dordrecht ; Boston : Kluwer, c1997.
QC611.98.H54F65 1997

[A]Balachandran A.P. [et al.].
Hubbard model and anyon superconductivity
Singapore ; Teaneck, NJ : World Scientific, c1990.
QC611.98.H54H83 1990

[A]Bartholomew, John, 1956-
Phase structure of a lattice superconductor
[microform]/ by John Bartholomew. 1983.
Microfilm 84/130 (Q)

[A]Basov, N. G
Elektronnye kharakteristiki i elektron-fononnye
English
Electronic characteristics and electron-phonon
interaction in superconducting metals and alloys / edited by
N. G. Basov ; translated from Russian by David L. Burdick.
New York : Consultants Bureau, c1977.
QC1.A4114 vol. 82; Alternative class.: QC612.S8

[A]Basov, N. G.
Nekotorye voprosy sverkhprovodimosti. English
Superconductivity / edited by;
translated from Russian by G. D. Archard.
New York : Consultants Bureau, c1977.
QC1.A4114 vol. 86; Alternative class.: QC612.S8

[A]Beenakker, C. W. J.; Random-matrix theory of quantum transport; Reviews of
Modern Physics.v. 69 July '97 p. 731-808.

A review of the statistical properties of the scattering matrix of a mesoscopic system is presented. This review is aimed at providing an up-to-date account of the area for physicists from outside the field. Topics discussed are quantum dots, disordered wires, and normal-metal-superconductor junctions.

[A]Benacka, S. , M. Darula, M. Kedro
International Symposium on Weak Superconductivity
(6th : 1991 : Smolenice, Slovakia)
Proceedings of the Sixth International Symposium
on Weak Superconductivity, Smolenice, Czechoslovakia, 20-24 May 1991.
Singapore ; River Edge, N.J. : World Scientific, c1991.
TK7872.S8I58 1991

[A]Benco, Lubomir; Barras, Jean Luc; Daul, Claude Auguste; Theoretical study of the intercalation of Li into TiO2 structures. Inorganic Chemistry.v. 38 no1 Jan. 11 '99 p. 20-8.
The interaction scheme constructed for spinel structures shows that electron density originating from intercalated Li atoms can be placed only on Ti atoms, which is confirmed by electron density plots. The difference density plots constructed for Li electron density only show that the occupation of d states due to the intercalation creates Ti-Ti (t2g-t2g) bonds in a more effective manner in the spinel than in the trigonal structure. This 3D t2g band is the electronic prerequisite for the superconductivity of the spinel LiTi2O4 compounds. Copyright 1999, American Chemical Society.

[A]Bogolëiìubov, N. N. (Nikola^i Nikolaevich), 1909- ed.
The theory of superconductivity.
New York, Gordon and Breach [1963, c1962]
QC612.S8B6213

[A]Bogolëiìubov, N. N. (Nikolaæi Nikolaevich), 1909-
The correlation functions in the theory of
superconductivity [by] N. N. Bogoliubov, Jr.
[Kiev, Nauk. dumka,] 1967.
QC612.S8B59

[A]Bogolëiìubov, N. N. (Nikolaæi Nikolaevich), 1909-
Uniform Title: Novyæi metod v teorii sverkhprovodimosti.
English
A new method in the theory of superconductivity
[by] N.N. Bogoliubov, V.V. Tolmachev, and D.V. Shirkov.
Translated from Russian.
New York, Consultants Bureau, 1959.
QC611.S8B613

[A]Bozovic, Ivan
Superconducting superlattices and multilayers :
24-25 January 1994, Los Angeles, California / Ivan Bozovic,
chair/editor ; sponsored and published by SPIE--the
International Society for Optical Engineering.
Bellingham, Wash., USA : SPIE, c1994.
QC611.94.S87 1994

[A]Buchanan, Mark; Daviss, Bennett; The heat is on; *New Scientist*.v. 154 May 3 '97 p. 26-9.
Theorists are currently arguing over the mechanism that produces high-temperature superconductivity. For the past 3 years, the "spin fluctuation theory" has been steadily gaining ground as a potential explanation of high-temperature superconductivity. However, in January 1997, evidence that Cooper pairs are made not from electrons but from polarons was found, rejuvenating a theory proposed in the early 1980s by Keith Johnson, in which the degeneracy that produces the polarons leads to the phonons being more effective at binding polarons together. Physicists are now starting to think that the real answer may be a combination of the phonon theory and spin fluctuation theory.

[A]Burnett, Keith; Go forth and multiply; *Science*.v. 282 no5394 Nov. 27 '98 p. 1657-8.
In this issue, Anderson and Kasevich demonstrate the Bose-Einstein equivalent of the familiar Josephson effect in superconductivity. In Bose-Einstein condensed systems, atoms enter a single macroscopic quantum state. The researchers directly observed macroscopic quantum oscillations in a waveform--phenomena known as Josephson effects, which rely on the ability of a macroscopic wave to extend over an object such as a small wall.

[A]Cahay, M.
International Symposium on Quantum Confinement
(2nd : 1994 : San Francisco, Calif.)
Proceedings of the Second International Symposium
on Quantum Confinement : physics and applications / editors,
M. Cahay ... [et al.].
Pennington, NJ : Electrochemcial Society, c1994.
TK7872.S8I5777 1994

[A]Cava, R. J.; Disorder in the ranks; Nature.v. 394 no6689 July 9 '98 p. 126-7.
The authors explain why changing the dopant in a high-temperature superconductor can greatly change the transition temperature (Tc). It has been over a decade since the first demonstrations of superconductivity in barium-doped La_2CuO_4 and in a strontium-doped analogue at a much higher temperature, but the great effect of the choice of dopant on Tc had thus far defied convincing explanation. They show that this effect is due to lattice strains, caused by disorder in the cation size: At a fixed hole concentration and lattice size, the extent of lattice-size disorder in the LaO layer has a strong effect on Tc, with

minimal size disorder producing the highest Tc.

[A]Chakravarty, Sudip; Quantum magnetism and its many avatars; Science.v. 278 Nov. 21 '97 p. 1412-13.
Although antiferromagnetism seems to abhor superconductivity and vice versa, the two are mysteriously linked. This situation would be intolerable but for clever and challenging experiments, such as the one reported by G. Aeppli et al. in this issue. The experiment hints at a novel state of matter linked to a quantum critical point and finds the existence of unusual magnetic scattering in a high-temperature superconductor, $La_{1.86}Sr_{0.14}CuO_4$, with a transition temperature of 35 K. The writer describes Aeppli et al.'s experiment and comments on its implications.

[A]Chern, S.S. C.W Chu, and C.S. Ting.
Physics and mathematics of anyons : proceedings
of the TCSUH Workshop, Houston, Texas, USA, 1-2 February 1991
/ [organized by Texas Center for Superconductivity,
University of Houston] ; edited by
Singapore ; Teaneck, N.J. : World Scietific, c1991.
QC611.98.A58T37 1991

[A]Chmaissem, O; Jorgensen, J. D; Short, S.; Scaling of transition temperature and CuO_2 plane buckling in a high-temperature superconductor. Nature.v. 397 no6714 Jan. 7 '99 p. 45-8.
Correlations between structure and transition temperature (Tc) in a superconducting compound with the "123" structure were studied. Observations of these structures, in which both under-doped and over-doped regimes could be accessed, revealed a clear scaling between Tc and the buckling of the copper oxide planes: Both went through a maximum at the same oxygen composition, implying a common origin. These and other findings indicated that, as the superconductor's composition is changed to increase Tc, there is a structural response that competes with the superconductivity.

[A]Chu, C. W; Xue, Y. Y; Du, Z. L.; Superconductivity up to 126 Kelvin in interstitially doped $Ba_2Ca_{n-1}Cu_nO_x$ (02(n-1)n-Ba); Science.v. 277 Aug. 22 '97 p. 1081-3.
A new high-temperature superconducting compound system, $Ba_2Ca_{n-1}Cu_nO_x$ [02(n-1) n-Ba] interstitially doped with calcium or (Ca,Cu) has been identified to exhibit a transition temperature up to 126 kelvin, the highest for a superconductor without a volatile toxic element. 02(n-1)n-Ba has body-centered tetragonal symmetry and an unusual charge-reservoir block.

[A]Coffey, Liam, 1958-
The interaction of superconductivity with
magnetism and localization [microform] / by Liam Coffey.1985.
Microfilm 86/880 (Q)

[A]Coleman, Piers; Opening the gap; Nature.v. 392 no6672 Mar. 12 '98 p. 134-5.
In this issue, Norman et al.'s angle-resolved photoemission study describes the collective motions of electrons in high-temperature superconductors. The study of underdoped Bi2212 at falling temperatures revealed a "pseudogap," or depletion of electrons, on the Fermi surface, breaking it up but leaving the shapes of the remaining arcs unchanged. Each arc was eaten away as the temperature was lowered further, until it finally vanished at the superconducting transition temperature.

[A]Crisan, M. (Mircea)
Theory of superconductivity / M. Crisan.
Singapore ; Teaneck, N.J. : World Scientific, c1989.
QC611.92.C75 1989
[A]Demiralp, Ersan; Goddard, William A., III.; Structures and energetics study of tetrathiafulvalene-based donors of organic superconductors; The Journal of Physical Chemistry A.v. 101 Oct. 23 '97 p. 8128-31.
The donors of the best organic superconductors are all based on organic donor molecules (X) containing a core of tetrathiafulvalene (TTF) or a Se-substituted derivative. In this paper, we present ab initio quantum mechanical calculations (HF, MP2, and DFT using the 6-31G** basis) for the optimized structures and other properties of TTF-based organic donors X and X+. The authors find that X+ is planar but that X deforms to a boat structure. The cases in which the boat is most stabilized with respect to the planar conformation are observed to be superconductors.

[A]Demiralp, Ersan; Goddard, William A.; Vibrational analysis and isotope shifts of BEDT-TTF donor for organic superconductors; The Journal of Physical Chemistry A.v. 102 no14 Apr. 2 '98 p. 2466-71.
Bis(ethylenedithio)tetrathiafulvalene (BEDT-TTF) is the best donor for 1-D and 2-D organic superconductors. Since coupling of vibrations with electronic states is critical to the nature of the superconductivity, it is essential to have a good understanding of the vibrational states. Many of the vibrational modes of BEDT-TTF were reported and assigned by Kozlov et al. and more were assigned by Eldridge et al., who made very complete isotope experiments. However, there remain several disagreements between these assignments. We report here the isotopic shifts for neutral BEDT-TTF based on ab initio calculations [Hartree-Fock (HF) using the 6-31G** basis set] for all fundamental vibrational frequencies. On the basis of these results, the authors propose new assignments for the fundamental vibrational frequencies of BEDT-TTF that satisfy the isotopic substitutions: (i) D for all H, (ii) 13C for the central carbons, (iii) 13C for all the double bond carbons, and (iv) 34S for all sulfurs.

[A]Demler, Eugene; Zhang, Shou Cheng; Quantitative test of a microscopic mechanism of high-temperature superconductivity; *Nature*.v. 396 no6713 Dec. 24-31 '98 p. 733-5.
A microscopic mechanism for the condensation energy of high-transition-temperature superconductors is proposed. The antiferromagnetic exchange energy in the superconducting state is lowered relative to the normal state within this mechanism due

to the appearance of a resonance in the superconducting state. The intensity of the resonant neutron-scattering peak observed previously in YBa2Cu3O7 during the transition to the superconducting state is in quantitative agreement with the condensation energy of these materials.

[A]Douçot , B. and J. Zinn-Justin
Fermions en forte interaction et
supraconductivité à haute température =
Strongly interacting fermions
and high Tc superconductivity
Amsterdam ; New York : Elsevier, 1995.
QC611.98.H54F47 1995

[A]Douglass, D. H.
Superconductivity in d- and f-band metals. Edited
by D. H. Douglass.
New York, American Institute of Physics, 1972.
QC612.S8S8

[A]Dresner, Lawrence.
Stability of superconductors / Lawrence Dresner.
New York : Plenum Press, c1995.
QC611.95.D74 1995

[A]Fujita, Shigeji.
Quantum statistical theory of superconductivity /
Shigeji Fujita and Salvador Godoy.
New York : Plenum Press, c1996.
QC611.92.F84 1996

[A]Fujita, Shigeji; Godoy, Salvador; Xian, Yang, reviewer; Quantum statistical theory of superconductivity (book review); Contemporary Physics.v. 39 no4 July/Aug. '98 p. 310-11.

[A]Fukuyama, H., S. Maekawa, and A.P. Malozemoff.
Strong correlation and superconductivity :
proceedings of the IBM Japan international symposium, Mt.
Fuji, Japan, 21-25 May, 1989 / editors,
Berlin ; New York : Springer-Verlag, c1989.
QC611.9.S77 1989

[A]Galasiewicz, Zygmunt M.
Superconductivity and quantum fluids, by Zygmunt
M. Galasiewicz.

Oxford, New York, Pergamon Press [1970]
QC612.S8G3 1970

[A]Gammel, Peter; Bishop, David; Fingerprinting vortices with smoke; Science.v. 279 Jan. 16 '98 p. 410-11.
A decade ago, the materials now called high-transition-temperature (high Tc) superconductors were discovered, seemingly heralding an imminent technological revolution. The abnormal behavior of magnetic fields, which form lattices of small vortices, has been a major impediment to successful applications of high Tc superconductors. The writers discuss the study of magnetic vortices using a simple and powerful technique called magnetic decoration.

[A]Gardiner, C. W. (Crispin W.), 1942-
Quantum noise / C.W. Gardiner.
Berlin ; New York : Springer-Verlag, c1991.
QC446.2.G37 1991

[A]Geesaman ,D.F.
Workshop on Hadron Structure Functions and Parton Distributions (1990 : Fermilab)
Proceedings of the Workshop on Hadron Structure Functions and Parton Distributions : Fermi National Accelerator Laboratory, 26-28 April 1990 / editors, D.F. Geesaman ... [et al.].
Singapore ; Teaneck, NJ : World Scientific, c1990.
QC793.5.H32W67 1990

[A]Geim, A. K; Dubonos, S. V; Lok, J. G. S.; Paramagnetic Meissner effect in small superconductors; Nature.v. 396 no6707 Nov. 12 '98 p. 144-6.
Small superconducting disks were studied to elucidate the origin of the paramagentic Meissner effect (PME). Numerous recent experiments have revealed that some superconducting samples may attract a magnetic field, the so-called PME. The results of the present study show that the PME is an oscillating function of the magnetic field and that it replaces the normal Meissner effect only above a certain field when several flux quanta are frozen inside a superconductor. The paramagnetic state is metastable. External noise restores the Meissner state.

[A]Geim, A. K; Grigorieva, I. V; Dubonos, S. V.; Phase transitions in individual sub-micrometre superconductors; Nature.v. 390 Nov. 20 '97 p. 259-62.
The magnetization of individual superconducting disks of diameters down to 100 nm was investigated using a new technique of ballistic Hall magnetometry. Little is known about what happens in small superconductors in the zero-resistance state. The superconducting state of these disks was qualitatively different from both macroscopic and microscopic superconductors. Specifically, these disks exhibited numerous phase transitions with properties that changed rapidly with size and temperature. This behavior was attributed to

the size quantization of the Cooper-pair motion and consequent transitions between discrete states of the superconducting Bose condensate in a magnetic field.

[A]Ginzburg , V.L.
Neravnovesnaëiìa sverkhprovodimost§. English.
Nonequilibrium superconductivity; translated by Kevin S. Hendzel.
Commack [N.Y.] : Nova Science Publishers, c1988.
QC1.A4114 vol. 174; Alternative class.: QC612.S8

[A]Ginzburg, V.L.(ed.)
Superconductivity, superdiamagnetism,
superfluidity; [translated from
Russian by Ram Wadhwa and Valerii Ilyushchenko].
Moscow : MIR Publishers, 1987.
QC611.92.S86 1987

[A]Gold, Alfred; Goldman, Allen M.; History of a quantum phase transition turns on a paradigm; Physics Today.v. 52 no3 Mar. '99 p. 115.
A letter responds to an article by A.M. Goldman and Nina Markovic on experiments that they interpreted as a superconductor-insulator transition. The writer asserts that Goldman and Markovic neglected to acknowledge his early contributions to theory about superconductor-insulator transitions, which predated the experimental results they discussed. Goldman replies.

[A]Goldman, Allen M; Markovic, Nina; Superconductor-insulator transitions in the two-dimensional limit; Physics Today.v. 51 no11 Nov. '98 p. 39-44.
The writer discusses topics, including disordered thin films, aspects of superconductivity, quantum phase transitions, the dirty-boson model, and the experimental situation.

[A]Golovashkin, A.I.
Perekhodnye proëtìsessy v sverkhprovodëiìashchikh
magnitnykh sistemakh / otvetstvennyæi redaktor toma A.I.
Golovashkin.
Moskva : Izd-vo "Nauka", 1984.
QC1.A4 t. 150; Alternative class.: QC761.3

[A]González, J.
Quantum electron liquids and high-Tc
superconductivity
Berlin ; New York : Springer, c1995.
QC611.98.H54Q3 1995

[A]Graham Rowe, Duncan; When Nobel dreams are too hot to handle: Augmented title: toxicity of high temperature superconductors; New Scientist.v. 159 no2153 Sept. 26 '98

p. 22.
A U.K. researcher has reported that a superconductor that keeps its zero resistance up to room temperature would probably be 10 times more toxic than cyanide. Plotting data on the toxicity of top high-temperature superconductors against the maximum temperatures at which they operate, Peter Edwards of the University of Birmingham found a strong relationship between the two. Specifically, he found that a superconductor operable at room temperature would have an LD50 of 0.4 mg/kg body weight.

[A]Gray, Kenneth E. (ed.)
NATO Advanced Study Institute on Nonequilibrium Superconductivity, Phonons, and Kapitza Boundaries (1980 : Acquafredda di Maratea, Italy)
Nonequilibrium superconductivity, phonons, and Kapitza boundaries
New York : Plenum Press published in cooperation with NATO Scientific Affairs Division, c1981.
QC612.S8N37 1980

[A]Gupta, L.C. (ed.)
Theoretical and experimental approaches to high-Tc and conventional superconductivity / editor, L.C. Gupta.
New York : Nova Science Publishers, 1991.
QC611.98.H54T48 1991

[A]Gurevich, A. Vl. (Aleksandr Vladimirovich), 1954-
Fizika kompozitnykh sverkhprovodnikov. English
The physics of composite superconductors / Alexander V. Gurevich, Roman G. Mints, and Alexander L. Rakhmanov ; translated from the Russian by S. Chomet.
Boca Raton, FL : CRC Press, 1995.
QC611.98.C63G8713 1995

[A]Gurevich, A. Vl. (Aleksandr Vladimirovich), 1954-
Fizika kompozitnykh sverkhprovodnikov. English
The physics of composite superconductors / A.V. Gurevich, R.G. Mints, A.L. Rakhmanov.
New York : Begell House, c1997.
QC611.98.C63G8713 1997

[A]Halley, J. Woods (editor).
Theories of high temperature superconductivity /
Redwood City, Calif. : Addison-Wesley Pub. Co., Advanced Book Program, c1988.
QC612.S8T48 1988

[A]Heppenheimer, T. A., 1947-
Superconductivity : research, applications &
potential markets / by T.A. Heppenheimer.
Arlington, Va. : Pasha Publications, [1987], c1988.
QC611.92.H47 1988

[A]Imaeda, Kenichi; Krober, Jonas; Nakano, Chikako; Recovery and enhancement of superconductivity in the sodium-hydrogen-C60 ternary system; The Journal of Physical Chemistry B.v. 101 Nov. 27 '97 p. 10136-40.
Sodium-hydrogen-C60 ternary compounds have been prepared by intercalation of sodium hydride (NaH) into C60. This method afforded a high-quality superconducting (SC) sample with a large volume fraction, but on the other hand, only a few high-quality SC samples were obtained and most of the samples were nonsuperconducting. However, we have succeeded in transforming a non-SC sample into an SC sample and in enhancing superconductivity. The Rietveld analysis clarifies that the non-SC phase (a-phase) has an orthorhombic structure, in contrast to a cubic structure for the SC phase (b-phase).

[A]Imamura, Yutaka; Ten no, Seiichiro; Tanimura, Yoshitaka;
Ab initio MO studies on electronic states of DCNQI molecules; The Journal of Physical Chemistry B.v. 103 no1 Jan. 7 '99 p. 266-70.
lectronic and geometrical structures of DR-DCNQI molecules (R = H, Cl, Br, I, Me, and OMe) were studied by performing ab initio MO calculations at the HF/DZP level. The authors carried out DCNQI monomer calculations and found that the optimized structures are close to experimental ones within errors of 0.04 A in a six-membered ring. They then discussed the basis set dependence of geometrical parameters and concluded that the polarization functions improve the description for double and triple bond states. Ab initio parameters such as transfer integrals were calculated for DCNQI dimers and trimers and compared with formerly calculated parameters. They found that the transfer integrals correlate well with lattice parameters of the c axis.

[A]Ishida, K; Mukuda, H; Kitaoka,Y.; Spin-triplet superconductivity in Sr2RuO4 identified by 17O knight shift; Nature.v. 396 no6712 Dec. 17 '98 p. 658-60.
Evidence that Cooper electron pairs in the layered oxide superconductor Sr2RuO4 can exist in a spin-triplet state is reported. Knight shift, as determined by 17O nuclear magnetic resonance, was used to determine the spin susceptibility of the Cooper pairs. There was no change in spin susceptibility on passing through the superconducting transition temperature, which demonstrates that Sr2RuO4 is a spin-triplet superconductor.

[A]Issledovaniëìa vysokovol'tnoæi izolëìaëtìsii
pri kriogennykh temperaturakh : [Sbornik stateæi / Otv. red.
d-r tekhn. nauk, prof. V. I. Levitov].
Moskva : çENIN, 1975.
TK3431.I77

[A]Jourdan, M; Huth, M; Adrian, H . Superconductivity mediated by spin fluctuations in the heavy-fermion compound UPd2Al3. Nature.v. 398 no6722 Mar. 4 '99 p. 47-9.

[A]Kawamoto, Atsushi; Taniguchi, Hiromi; Kanoda, Kazushi; Superconductor-insulator transition controlled by partial deuteration in BEDT-TTF salt; Journal of the American Chemical Society.v. 120 no42 Oct. 28 '98 p. 10984-5.
The partial deuteration of BEDT-TTF molecules provides a means of controlling the system with minimal inhomogeneity and to turn it finely around the M-I transition. The partial deuteration of the organic superconductor k-(BEDT-TTF)2Cu[N(CN)2]Br allows the molecular arrangement in the 2-D BEDT-TTF sheet to be controlled so finely that the bandwidth of the system crosses the critical value of the Mott transition.

[A]Klein, M. V; Blumberg, G.; Effective mass and color change; Science.v. 283 no5398 Jan. 1 '99 p. 42-3.
In this issue, Basov and colleagues report new data on high-transition temperature superconductors. These data demonstrate how such non-conventional superconductors atypically obey a sum rule, which is an exact expression that relates sums of measured quantities to known parameters.

[A]Kobayashi, Hayao; Sato, Akane; Arai, Emiko; Superconductor-to-insulator transition in an organic metal incorporating magnetic anions: l-(IBETS)2(FexGa1-X)Cl4 (BETS = bis(ethylenedithio)tetraselenafulvalene; x (similar) 0.55 and 0.43); Journal of the American Chemical Society.v. 119 Dec. 17 '97 p. 12392-3.
Crystals of l-(BETS)2(FexGa1 - x)Cl4 (1), where BETS = bis(ethylenedithio)tetraselenafulvalene, were characterized. Resistivity and magnetic susceptibility measurements demonstrated the existence of a superconducting transition and a subsequent, unprecedented superconductor-to-insulator transition. Magnetic Fe3+ ions were found to play an essential role in the latter transition.

[A]Kockerling, Martin; Johrendt, Dirk; Finckh, E. Wolfgang; Superconductivity in Nb21S8, a phase with metal cluster chains; Journal of the American Chemical Society.v. 120 no47 Dec. 2 '98 p. 12297-302.
Phase pure samples of Nb21S8 are obtained by chemical transport and molten flux reactions in sealed niobium containers at 850-950 [degree]C. In the temperature range from 5 to 290 K the electrical conductivity is found to be moderate metallic with a specific resistivity of 3.90 mQ cm at 273 K. Magnetic susceptibility measurements give weak, almost temperature independent paramagnetism above [similar] 40 K. These metallic properties are compared with the structure of Nb21S8, which contains linear single and double chains of fused body centered niobium cubes, separated by S and additional Nb atoms. Both physical measurements consistently show a transition into the superconducting state below 4.1(5) and 3.7(2) K, respectively.

[A]Kresin , Vladimir Z. and William A. Little.
International Conference on Organic

Superconductivity (1990 : South Lake Tahoe, Calif.)
Organic superconductivity / edited by
New York : Plenum Press, c1990.
QC611.98.O74I57 1990

[A]Krusin Elbaum, L; Lopez, D; Thompson, J. R.; Superconductivity enhanced by Hg fission; Nature.v. 389 Sept. 18 '97 p. 243-4.
A technique that enhances the superconductivity of high-temperature copper oxide superconductors is described. The successful application of such superconductors requires a solution to the problem of the ease of motion of magnetic vortices, or quantized flux lines, that results in finite electrical resistance and prevents loss-free conduction of current. This problem can be overcome by the fission of mercury atoms in a mercury/copper oxide superconductor. The fission of the mercury induces crystallographic defects that anchor the magnetic vortices.

[A]Kuper, Charles Goethe.
An introduction to the theory of
superconductivity, by Charles G. Kuper.
Oxford, Clarendon P., 1968.
QC612.S8K86

[A]Kvantovo-polevye metody issledovaniëìa
sverkhprovodëìashchikh i normal'nykh sistem /
[redakëtìsionnaëìa kollegiëìa P.I. Khadzhi (otvetstvennyæi
redaktor) ... et al.].
Kishinev : "Shtiinëtìsa", 1988.
MLCS 95/10028 (Q)

[A]Langenberg, D.N. , and A.I. Larki(eds.)
Nonequilibrium superconductivity / volume
Amsterdam ; New York : North-Holland ; New York,
N.Y. : Sole distributors for the U.S.A. and Canada, Elsevier
Science, 1986.
QC612.S8N66 1986

[A]Lee, David M.; The extraordinary phases of liquid 3He; Reviews of Modern Physics.v. 69 July '97 p. 645-65.
The address given by David M. Lee on his receipt of the 1996 Nobel Prize in Physics, which he was jointly awarded with Douglas D. Osheroff and Robert C. Richardson, is presented. Lee discusses the remarkable phases of liquid 3He. The different ways in which superfluid 3He research can be linked to high-Tc superconductivity, heavy-fermion superconductivity, and liquid crystals in condensed matter physics were investigated.

[A]Lengeler, H.(ed.)
Workshop on RF-Superconductivity (2nd : 1984 :
Geneva, Switzerland)
Proceedings of the Second Workshop on
RF-Superconductivity : Geneva, Switzerland, July 23-27, 1984
[Geneva] : European Organization for Nuclear
Research, [1984]
QC612.S8W67 1984

[A]Leon Rossano, L. M. An inexpensive and easy experiment to measure the electrical resistance of high-Tc superconductors as a function of temperature; American Journal of Physics.v. 65 Oct. '97 p. 1024-6.
A simple method was employed to vary the temperature of high-Tc superconductors from room temperature to liquid nitrogen temperatures. A standard 4-point technique was used to measure the electrical resistance as a function of temperature. The method required no more than 2 liters of liquid nitrogen and allowed the measurement of metal-superconductor transition of the high-Tc superconductors.

[A]Liu, R. S; Chang, C. Y; Chen, J. M.; Hole distribution in underdoped and overdoped Y(Ba2-ySry)Cu3O6+d compounds studied by X-ray absorption spectroscopy; Inorganic Chemistry.v. 37 no21 Oct. 19 '98 p. 5527-31.
The hole distribution of underdoped and overdoped states in the Y(Ba2-ySry)Cu3O6+d (d [similar] 0.1 and 0.9) compounds has been observed by high-resolution O K-edge X-ray-absorption near-edge-structure spectra. The chemical substitution of Sr for Ba in the fully oxygenated Y(Ba2-ySry)Cu3O6+d (d [similar] 0.9) compounds gives rise to high hole concentrations within both the CuO2 planes and the out-of-plane sites, leading to the overdoped state and the decrease in the superconducting transition temperature from 92 K for y = 0 to 84 K for y = 0.8.

[A]Lüders, Gerhart.
The method of the correlation function in
superconductivity theory [by] G. Lüders and K.-D. Usadel.
[Berlin, New York, Springer-Verlag, 1971]
QC1.S797 Bd. 56; Alternative class.: QC612.S8

[A]Lundqvist, S. et al.
Adriatico Research Conference and Workshop on
Towards the Theoretical Understanding of High Tc
Superconductors (1988 : International Center for Theoretical Physics)
Proceedings of the Adriatico Research Conference
and Workshop on Towards the Theoretical Understanding of High
Tc Superconductors, ICTP, Trieste, Italy, 20 June-29 July 1988
Singapore ; Teaneck, N.J. : World Scientific, c1988.
QC611.98.H54A36 1988

[A]Lynn, Jeffrey W.(ed.)
High temperature superconductivity
with contributions by Philip B. Allen ...
New York : Springer-Verlag, c1990.
QC611.98.H54H5433 1990

[A]Lynton, E. A. (Ernest Albert)
Superconductivity [by] E.A. Lynton.
London, Methuen; New York, Wiley [1964]
QC612.S8L9 1964

[A]Lynton, E. A. (Ernest Albert)
Superconductivity.
London, Methuen; New York, Wiley [1962]
QC612.S8L9

[A]Mathur, N. D; Burnell, G; Isaac, S. P.; Large low-field magnetoresistance in La0.7Ca0.3MnO3 induced by artificial grain boundaries; Nature.v. 387 May 15 '97 p. 266-8.
The influence of specific structural defects on the colossal magnetoresistance (CMR) behavior of La0.7Ca0.3MnO3 was investigated. CMR refers to the phenomenon in which compounds demonstrate very large changes in electrical resistance when a magnetic field is applied. Thin film devices were constructed that isolated the contribution of a single grain boundary that was introduced into an epitaxial film of La0.7Ca0.3MnO3 by growing the compound on a bicrystal substrate.

[A]Moler, Kathryn A; Kirtley, John R; Hinks, D. G.; Images of interlayer Josephson vortices in Tl2Ba2CuO6+d; Science.v. 279 no5354 Feb. 20 '98 p. 1193-6.
The strength of the interlayer Josephson tunneling in layered superconductors is an essential test of the interlayer tunneling model as a mechanism for superconductivity, as well as a useful phenomenological parameter. A scanning superconducting quantum interference device (SQUID) microscope was used to image interlayer Josephson vortices in Tl2Ba2CuO6+d and to obtain a direct measure of the interlayer tunneling in a high-transition temperature superconductor with a single copper oxide plane per unit cell.

[A]Nagaoka, K; Yamashita, T; Uchiyama, S.; Monochromatic electron emission from the macroscopic quantum state of a superconductor; Nature.v. 396 no6711 Dec. 10 '98 p. 557-9.
Field-emission experiments were used to examine the theoretical prediction that monochromatic electrons are emitted from a superconductor into a vacuum. The results confirm the emission of monochromatic electron beams. Emissions of this type may possibly find application as the sources in a range of electron-based spectroscopies.

[A]Noce , C., A. Romano, and G. Scarpetta
Superconductivity and strongly correlated electron systems:
Amalfi, Italy, 14-16 October 1993 /
Singapore ; River Edge, N.J. : World Scientific, c1994.
QC611.98.H54S88 1994

[A]Ozhogina, V.I.
Sverkhprovodimost' = Superconductivity : sbornik
stateæi / pod redakëtìsieæi.
Moskva : ëTìSNIIatominform, 1987.

[A]Parks, R. D., 1935-
Superconductivity, edited by R. D. Parks.
New York, M. Dekker, 1969.
QC612.S8P28

[A]Phillips, J. C.; Filamentary microstructure and linear temperature dependence of normal state transport in optimized high temperature superconductors; Proceedings of the National Academy of Sciences of the United States of America.v. 94 Nov. 25 '97 p. 12771-5.
A filamentary model of "metallic" conduction in layered cuprate high-temperature superconductors is presented. The new model accounts for the concurrence of normal state resistivities that are linear in temperature with optimized superconductivity and predicts the lowest temperature for which linearity holds and the maximum superconductive transition temperature. The theory behind the new model abandons the effective medium approximation that includes Fermi liquids and other nonpercolative models in favor of countable smart basis states.

[A]Rice, Maurice; An analogue of superfluid 3He; Nature.v. 396 no6712 Dec. 17 '98 p. 627-9.
A complete description of the unconventional superconductivity of strontium ruthenate (Sr2RuO4) is now available. Articles by Luke et al. and Riseman et al. (1998;396:558-61 and 242-5, respectively) in previous issues and a report by Ishida et al. in this issue have established that the superconductivity of Sr2RuO4 conforms to long-held views on how superconductivity driven by electron-electron interactions should behave.

[A]Rickayzen, G.
Theory of superconductivity [by] G. Rickayzen.
New York, Interscience Publishers [1965]
QC612.S8R5

[A]Riseman, T. M; Kealey, P. G; Forgan, E. M.; Observation of a square flux-line lattice in the unconventional superconductor Sr2RuO4; Nature.v. 396 no6708 Nov. 19 '98 p. 242-5.

The observation of a square magnetic-flux-line lattice in the unconventional perovskite superconductor Sr2RuO4 (SRO) is reported. SRO has almost 2-D metallic properties with a well-established Fermi surface that consists of three sheets: a, b, and c. Magnetic flux lines in SRO formed a square lattice over a wide range of fields and temperatures, as predicted by a recent theory of p-wave superconductivity in this substance.

[A]Rodgers, Peter; Theory debate gets literary, and ugly; Science.v. 281 no5382 Sept. 4 '98 p. 1427.
A research paper presented in a recent issue of Physical Review Letters has sparked controversy in the field of high-temperature superconductivity (HTS). The paper claimed that bipolaron theory cannot predict superconducting transition temperatures above 10 kelvin, which is too low to explain the phenomenon of HTS. What is more, it closed by comparing the bipolaron theory to cartoon figures that continue to enjoy charmed lives until the celluloid runs out.

[A]Rose-Innes, Alistair Christopher.
Introduction to superconductivity / by A. C.
Rose-Innes and E. H. Rhoderick.
Oxford ; New York : Pergamon Press, c1969, 1976
printing.
QC612.S8R6 1976

[A]Rose-Innes, Alistair Christopher.
Introduction to superconductivity / by A. C.
Rose-Innes and E. H. Rhoderick.
Oxford ; New York : Pergamon Press, 1978.
QC612.S8R6 1978

[A]S. Benacka and M. Kedro (Eds.)
Weak Superconductivity
290 pages, 1990. $135. ISBN 0-941743-78-0.
Superconductivity; Physics; Materials Science; Chemistry; Electronics.
Partial Contents: Some Aspects of D.C. Magnetron Sputtering of YBaCuO Thin Films; •DC Magnetron Sputtering of Yttrium and Bismuth Based High-Tc Films; •Superconducting Bi-Sr-Ca-Cu-O Thin Films Prepared by RF Magnetron Sputtering and their Chemical Patterning; •In-Situ Preparation of High-Quality $YBa_2Cu_3O_{7-x}$ Films on $SrTiO_3$ Substrates by Laser Ablation; •Magnetron and Laser-Beam Methods of HTSC Thin Film Deposition; •Properties of YBaCuO Superconducting Thin Films Deposited by Nitrogen Laser Evaporation and Heat-Treated in O_2 Atmosphere by CW CO_2 - Laser; •The Influence of BaO and Ba on the Process of Vacuum Coevaporation and Properties of Y-Ba-Cu-O Thin Films; •The Auger Electron Spectroscopy Studies of Y-Ba-Cu-O Thin Film - Substrate Diffusion Interface; •Critical Current Densities of Polycrystalline $YBa_2Cu_3O_x$ Thin Films in Magnetic Fields up to 9T;

[A]Sa de Melo, Carlos A.R.
The superconducting state in magnetic fields :
special topics and new trends / Carlos A.R. Sa de Melo.
River Edge, N.J. : World Scientific, 1998.
QC173.458.M33S86 1998

[A]Saint-James, D., 1927-
Type II superconductivity [by] D. Saint-James,
and G. Sarma, [and] E. J. Thomas.
Oxford, New York, Pergamon Press [1969]
QC612.S8S2 1969

[A]Savchenko, M. A.
Fluktuaëtìsionnaëiìa sverkhprovodimost'
magnitnykh sistem. English
Fluctuational superconductivity of magnetic
systems / M.A. Savchenko, A.V. Stefanovich ; [translators,
Ram S. Wadhwa, Natalie Wadhwa].
Berlin ; New York : Springer-Verlag, c1990.
QC761.3.S2813 1990

[A]Schechter, Bruce.
The path of no resistance : the story of the
revolution in superconductivity / Bruce Schechter.
New York : Simon and Schuster, c1989.
QC611.95.S34 1989

[A]Schrieffer, J. R. (John Robert), 1931-
Theory of superconductivity [by] J.R. Schrieffer.
New York, W.A. Benjamin, 1964.
QC612.S8S3

[A]Schrieffer, J. R. (John Robert), 1931-
Theory of superconductivity / J.R. Schrieffer.
Reading, Mass. : Benjamin/Cummings Pub. Co., [1983]
QC612.S8S3 1983

[A]Schrieffer, J. R.
Theory of superconductivity / J. R. Schrieffer.
Reading, MA : Perseus Books, 1999.
9903 BOOK NOT YET IN LC

[A]Seife, Charles; Cold reception for superconductivity claim; New Scientist.v. 159
no2143 July 18 '98 p. 12.

Deborah Chung, a materials scientist at the State University of New York at Buffalo, has claimed she can make everyday circuits that are superconducting at room temperature by combining negative resistors with normal conductors. The negative resistors are formed by setting small carbon fibers into epoxy at high temperatures. Researchers remain to be convinced and contend that while negative resistance is real, it has only been observed at higher voltages.

[A]Service, Robert F.; Could charge stripes be a key to superconductivity? Science.v. 283 no5405 Feb. 19 '99 p. 1106-8.
Charge stripes could be a key to superconductivity. Charges flow back and forth through high-temperature superconductors in a series of stripes a few atoms wide, fashioning a landscape that helps current flow effortlessly through the material in all directions. The writer discusses the discovery of stripes and the debate about their significance.

[A]Shimizu, K; Suhara, K; Ikumo, M.; Superconductivity in oxygen; Nature.v. 393 no6687 June 25 '98 p. 767-9.
The superconductive ability of oxygen was investigated. Oxygen exhibits magnetism at low temperatures, and at pressures exceeding 95 GPa, solid molecular oxygen becomes metallic and undergoes a structural transition. At pressures of approximately 100 GPa, solid oxygen became superconducting and had a transition temperature of 0.6 K. This transition was detected by both resistivity measurements and a Meissner demagnetization signal.

[A]Sigrist, Manfred; Mesoscopic magnetism; Nature.v. 396 no6707 Nov. 12 '98 p. 110-11.
The authors present measurements made on superconducting aluminum disks as small as 0.3 mm across that show superconductors to have a peculiar attraction for magnetic fields. This "paramagnetic Meissner effect" has been suggested to apply only to superconductors that are somehow unconventional, but the observations contradict such claims, as their aluminum disks are conventional superconductors. In their mesoscopic system, paramagnetism arises from metastable magnetic states that occur with a large number of vortex patterns.

[A]Stabilité des supraconducteurs en hélium I et
hélium II : compte rendu des journées de Saclay (France) =
Stability of superconductors in helium I and helium II :
proceedings of the workshop held at Saclay (France) : Nov.
16-19, 1981.
Paris : Institut international du froid, 1981.
QC761.3.S68 1981

[A]Struzhkin Viktor, V; Hemley, Russell J; Mao, Ho kwang; Superconductivity at 10-17 K in compressed sulphur; Nature.v. 390 Nov. 27 '97 p. 382-4.
A study explored the possibility of superconductivity in a material at very high pressures.

At 93 GPa, elemental sulfur was seen to transform not only to a metal but to a superconductor with a transition temperature, Tc, of 10.1 K. Tc was found to increase linearly with pressure up to 157 GPa, in contrast with the negative dTc/dP seen in the heavier superconducting chalcogenides selenium and tellurium. Furthermore, at the transformation in sulfur to a higher pressure metallic phase near 160 GPa, Tc increases from 14 K to 17 K.

[A]Studies of High Temperature Superconductors. Volume 14.
Field Penetration and Magnetization of High Temperature Superconductors
Anant Narlikar (Ed.)
445 Pp. 1994. . ISBN 1-56072-182-0. $110
Contents: Preface; • Chapter-L: Visualization Of Shubnikov Phase Using The High Resolution Faraday Effect (Th. Schuster); • Chapter-2: Mechanism Of Microwave Absorption And Flux Distribution In High Temperature Superconductors (T. Endo And H. Yan); • Chapter-3: Field Penetration And Magnetization Of Hts (S. Senoussi, S. Hammond,f. Mosbah); • Chapter-4: Experimental Aspects Of Magnetization Studies In Superconductors (A.K. Grover); • Chapter-5: Recent Developments Of The Critical State Model (P. Chaddah); • Chapter-6: Anomalous Magnetization In Ybacuo Single Crystals; Surface Barrier And Fish-Tail (Ming Xu, K. Zhang And B. Bobowski); • Chapter-7: Low Field Magnetic Behaviour Of High Temperature Superconductors (F. De La Cruz, H. Pastoriza And A. Arribere); • Chapter-8: Irreversible Part Of Magnetization Due To Flux Pinning (K. Yamafuji); • Chapter-9: Irreversibility Line In High Temperature Superconductors (T. Matsushita); • Chapter-10: Non-Linear Flux Flow Regime In High Temperature Superconductors (S.Takacs And F. Gomory); Chapter-Ll: Harmonic Generation In High Tc Superconductors; (Neeraj Khare And A.K. Gupta); • Subject Index.

[A]Studies of High Temperature Superconductors. Volume 6
A.V. Narlikar (Ed.)
1990. 413 pages, $150. ISBN 0-941743-88-8.
Superconductivity, Physics, Chemistry, Materials Science, Solid State Electronics, Engineeering
Contents: •High Temperature Superconductors - Crystal Growth and Characterization; •Anisotropic Properties of Single Crystals of High Tc Superconductors; •Anomalous Transport Properties of HTSC Thin Films; •Organic Superconductors - Prospects for High Tc; •Electronic Structure Studies of High-Tc Cuprate Superconductors by Electron Energy-Loss Spectroscopy; •Polaron Theory of High-Tc Strong-Coupling Superconductors; •Response Function Characteristics of Pairing Correlations in the New High-Tc Superconductors; •Electric Field Effect on Epidxial $Y_1Ba_2Cu_3O_y$ Films; •Flux Penetration into High Tc Superconductors in AC Magnetic Fields; •Preparation Methods of Polycrystalline $YBa_2Cu_3O_7$: Influence on the Superconducting Properties; •Carrier Dependent Superconductivity in Cuprates.

[A]Studies of High Temperature Superconductors. Volume 8
A.V. Narlikar (Ed.)
414 pages, 1992. $150 . ISBN 1-56072-019-0.
Superconductivity; Physics Chemistry; Materials Science; Solid State Engineering
Contents: Metal-Insulator Transitions, Exchange Interactions and Real Space Pairing (An Introduction to the Theory of Strongly Correlated Electron Systems); Magnetic Properties of R_2CuO_4 Materials; CVD Route for High Jc Superconductors; HTSC Thick Films: Their Synthesis, Structure, Properties and Applications; Vibrating - Reed Studies on High-Tc Superconductors; Magnetic Ordering in $YBa_2Cu_3O_{6+x}$ and Related Systems; Electronic Structure and Correlation Effects in HTSC; Superconducting Fluctuation Effect in HTSCs; Strong-Coupling Interaction in High-Tc Superconductors; Positron Annihilation in High Temperature Superconductors; On the Anomalous Magnetic Behaviors of High-Tc Oxide Superconductors - Are They Really Anomalous?

[A]Studies of High Temperature Superconductors. Volume 9
Anant Narlikar (Ed.)
331 pages. 1992. ISBN 1-56072-061-1. $145.
Superconductivity; Physics; Chemistry; Materials Science; Solid State Engineering
Contents: Flux Pinning of Melt Processed YBCO Superconductors and Their Applications; Neutron Irradiation Effects in High Tc Single Crystals; Redox Mechanisms in High Tc Superconductive Cuprates; Thermal Expansion and Gruneisen Parameters of High Tc Superconductors; Processing Dependent Parameters of Tl-Ca-Ba-Cu-O High Tc Compounds; Magnetic Field Dependent Microwave Absorption in High Temperature Superconductors; Isotope Effect in Superconducting Perovskites; Tunneling Spectroscopy on High Tc Superconductors; Epitaxial Heterostructures for High Tc Superconducting Electronics.

[A]Superconductivity: Theoretical and Experimental Effects
K.N. Shrivastava (Ed.)
1996, 327 pp., ISBN 1-56072-360-2. $95.
This state-of-the-art volume brings together leading researchers on superconductivity. New discoveries and approaches are represented.
Contents: 1. Combined phononic and lochonic mechanism and isotope effect in cuprate superconductors. 2. Symmetry considerations in an electronic mechanism of superconductivity.; 3. Vortex overlapping: Magnetisation and specific heat of high temperature superconductors.; 4. Strongly correlated electron systems.; 5. A phenomenological theory of a high Tc superconductor with coexisting magnetic order.; 6. Detection of x-rays by pair breaking in superconductors..; 7. The effect of electric field on superconductors..8. Normal state resistivity of highly correlated Bi2Sr2CaCu2O8+x. 9. Carbon superconductors..; 10. Low temperature specific heat and related studies on pure and substitute phases of high Tc cuprates.; 11. Microwave surface resistance of HTSC thin films. 12. Observation of hysteretic to flux-flow transition in Xac of HTSCs.; 13. Specific heat superconductors.; 15. AC susceptibility in sintered superconducting

doped W/Mo and undoped (Bi,Pb -2223).; 16. Imaginary ac susceptibility in superconducting BiPbMoSrCaCuO.; 17. Penetration depth in high-Tc superconductors.; 18. Microwave measurements of granular superconductors..; 19. Word Index.

[A]Superconductors with A15 Lattice and Bridge
Contacts Based Upon Them
M.M. Sushchinskiy, (Ed.)
354 pp., 1991. (Vol. 190. Supl. Vol.-Proc. of the Lebedev Physics Inst.). $135. ISBN 1-56072-011-5
Superconductivity; Solid State Physics; Cryogenics This volume is devoted to an investigation of the physical characteristics of a number of high-temperature superconducting compounds and to an investigation of the properties of certain electronic components based on these compounds. The correlation of the critical temperature, Tc, of superconductors with their electron, phonon, atomic and structural properties is analyzed. The issue of the ultimate possibilities for enhancement of the critical parameters of superconductors within the framework of the phonon superconductivity mechanism is discussed..Contents: Relationship of Critical Temperature with Physical Characteristics of Superconductors; Superconducting Nb_3Ge and Nb_3Si Compounds; Optical Modulation Spectroscopy and Electronic Structure of Metals and Alloys.

[A]Tanaka, Hisashi; Kobayashi, Akiko; Sato, Akane; Chemical control of electrical properties and phase diagram of a series of l-type BETS superconductors, l-(BETS)2GaBrxCl4-x Journal of the American Chemical Society.v. 121 no4 Feb. 3 '99 p. 760-8.
The crystal structure determinations of a series of l-(BETS)2GaBrxCl4-x and the calculations of the intermolecular overlap integrals of the highest occupied molecular orbital of BETS were made to elucidate a key factor of the superconducting transition mechanism. The x-dependence of intermolecular overlap integrals seems to suggest that the magnitude of the "spin gap" of the nonmagnetic insulating state tends to be diminished with decreasing x. There exists one intermolecular overlap integral exhibiting a large temperature and x-dependence, which seems to play a crucial role in determining the nature of the ground state.

[A]Theoretical and Experimental Approaches to High Tc and Conventional Superconductivity
L.C. Gupta (Ed.)
810 pages, 1991. $175. ISBN 1-56072-009-3.
Superconductivity; Materials Science; Chemistry; Solid State Physics
Partial Contents: A Child's Guide to BCS; Competing Bonds in High-Tc Superconductors; The Statistical Distribution of the Thermal Energy; Conductivity and Superconductivity; Critical Indices for High-Tc Superconductors; Role of Redox Ions and Apex Oxygen in Enhancement of Tc of New Oxide Superconductors; Charged Bose Gas Model for High-Tc Superconductors; Ginzburg-Landau Phenomenology for High-Tc

Systems; Microscopic Theory of Layered High-Tc Superconductors; Phenomenolgy Constraints on Theories for High-Tc Superconductivity;

[A]Thermodynamics and Electrodynamics of Superconductors
V.L. Ginzburg (Ed.)
294 pp., 1988. (Vol. 174 Supl.Vol. 1 Proc. of the Lebedev Physics Inst.). $145. ISBN 0-941743-18-7.
Superconductivity
This volume is devoted to an investigation of superconductivity: one of the most important fields in solid state physics. This volume contains research on electron-phonon interaction in equilibrium and nonequilibrium superconductors and considers the problem of the coexistence of behavior of a Josephson junction of finite width with magnetic field current is investigated and frequency synthesis in superconducting and weakly-coupled systems is examined.

[A]Tilley, David R.
Superfluidity and superconductivity / David R. Tilley, John Tilley.
Bristol ; Boston : A. Hilger ; Brighton :
Published in association with the University of Sussex Press, c1986.
QC175.4.T54 1986

[A]Tilley, David R.
Superfluidity and superconductivity [by] David R. Tilley and John Tilley.
New York, Wiley [1974]
QC175.4.T54

[A]Tilley, David R; Tilley, John, 1939 ; Superfluidity and superconductivity (book review) Leggett, A. J., reviewer Nature.v. 398 no6722 Mar. 4 '99 p. 38.

[A]Tinkham, Michael
Superconductivity [by] M. Tinkham.
New York, Gordon and Breach [1966, c1965]
QC612.S8T5 1966

[A]Tsvetkov, A. A; van der Marel, D; Moler, K. A.; Global and local measures of the intrinsic Josephson coupling in Tl2Ba2CuO6 as a test of the interlayer tunnelling model; Nature.v. 395 no6700 Sept. 24 '98 p. 360-2.
Global and local measures of the intrinsic Josephson coupling in the high-temperature superconductor Tl2Ba2CuO6 were examined as a test of the tunneling model. One leading candidate theory of high-temperature superconductivity in the copper oxide systems is the interlayer tunneling (ILT) mechanism, which purports that superconductivity is created by tunneling of electron pairs between copper oxide planes. Both the sample-averaging optical probe and local vortex imaging in Tl2Ba2CuO6 gave a consistent value of qJ [approximately equal to] 28 cm-1.

[A]Urban, Eugene Willard.
Magnetic flux flow in a type II superconductor.
Washington, National Aeronautics and Space
Administration; [for sale by the National Technical
Information Service, Springfield, Va.]1971.
TL521.A3525 no. 6244; Alternative class.:
QC612.S8

[A]Veldhuizen, Yvonne S. J; Smeets, Wilberth J. J; Veldman, Nora; Synthesis and characterization of (acridinium)(Ni(dmit)2)3 and (phenazinium)(Ni(dmit)2)3 (dmit = 2-thioxo-1,3-dithiole-4,5-dithiolate); Inorganic Chemistry.v. 36 Oct. 22 '97 p. 4930-7.

[A]von Baeyer, Hans Christian; Tiny doubles; The Sciences.v. 37 Sept./Oct. '97 p. 11-13. Individual bosons and electrons are indistinguishable from each other, and a phenomenon called Bose-Einstein condensation (BEC) allows huge numbers of such atomic constituents cooperating with each other to elevate subtle quantum effects to macroscopic scale, producing remarkable effects. Examples of phenomena resulting from BEC include superconductivity, superfluidity, and BEC in a gas, all of which constitute new phases of matter. Recent research into BEC is discussed.

[A]Vysokotemperaturnaëiìa sverkhprovodimost' =
hightemperature superconductivity : fundam. i prikl. issled :
sb. nauch. st.
Leningrad : Mashinostroenie Leningr. otd-nie, 1990.

[A]Weber, Harald W.
Supraleitung = Superconductivity / von H.W. Weber
und O. Hittmair.
München : K. Thiemig, c1979.
QC612.S8W43 1979

[A]Wells, B. O; Lee, Y. S; Kastner, M. A.; Incommensurate spin fluctuations in high-transition temperature superconductors; Science.v. 277 Aug. 22 '97 p. 1067-71. Neutron scattering experiments have revealed a fascinating interplay between the hole doping, the spin fluctuations, and the superconductivity of the cuprate superconductors. Recently, electrochemical techniques have been used to produce large single crystals of La2CuO4+y, which has mobile oxygen dopants. Staging behavior of the excess oxygen has been demonstrated, and the low-energy spin fluctuations in stage 6 La2CuO4+y have been measured. The spin fluctuations are incommensurate with the lattice and have spatial, energy, and temperature dependencies very much like those in La2-xSrxCuO4, with similar high transition temperature.

[A]Widrow, Lawrence M. (Lawrence Marc), 1962-
Zero modes and anomalies in superconducting

strings [microform]/ by Lawrence M. Widrow. 1988.
Microfilm 92/511 (Q)

[A]Wilczek, Frank.
Fractional statistics and anyon superconductivity
Frank Wilczek.
Singapore ; Teaneck, NJ : World Scientific, c1990.
QC611.98.H54W55 1990

[A]Wolf , Stuart A. and Vladimir Z. Kresin.
International Workshop on Novel Mechanisms of
Superconductivity (1987 : Berkeley, Calif.)
Novel superconductivity
New York : Plenum Press, c1987.
QC612.S8I57 1987

[A]Yeshurun, Yosef.
Agirat energyah bi-selilim molikhe °al
be-òtemperaòturot gevohot : duaòh sofi shel shenat
ha-meòhòkar ha-rishonah / Yosef Yeshurun.
Medinat Yiâsra'el : Miâsrad ha-energyah
òveha-tashtit, Agaf meòhòkar u-fituaòh, [1995]
TK2985.Y47 1995

[A]Yoshizawa, Kazunari; Kato, Takashi; Tachibana, Masamitsu Vibronic interactions in silicon polyhedra of the Si46 clathrate compound The Journal of Physical Chemistry A.v. 102 no49 Dec. 3 '98 p. 10113-19.
The vibronic (vibrational-electronic) interactions in the Si46 clathrate compound are discussed using the highly symmetric (SiH)20 and (SiH)24 cluster models to look at a possible correlation between the Jahn-Teller effect and the superconductivity. The vibronic coupling constants for six Hg modes in the mono-, tri-, and pentaanions of (SiH)20 and for twelve E4 modes in the tri- and pentaanions of (SiH)24 are calculated using the MNDO-PM3 method, one of the most reliable semiempirical molecular orbital methods, to know which mode of vibration plays a governing role in the Jahn-Teller distortions of these interesting hypothetical multianions.

[A]Zusman, Leonid D; Beratan, David N; Structure of the electrical double layer in high-temperature superconductors. Origin of the dip in the double-layer capacitance near the superconducting transition; The Journal of Physical Chemistry B.v. 101 Sept. 4 '97 p. 7095-9.
A theory of the electrical double layer in high-temperature superconductors is developed in the context of a modified Ginzburg-Landau equation. Potential and excess charge distributions inside the electrode are computed. These distributions are shown to be characterized by a new fundamental length parameter. The dependence of this capacitance dip on the external field is predicted.

Devices

[B]A. Barone, R. Cristiano, S.Pagano
X-ray detection by superconducting tunnel
junctions : proceedings of the workshop, Naples, Italy, 12-14
December 1990 / edited by A. Barone, R. Cristiano, S.
Pagano.
Singapore ; River Edge, NJ : World Scientific, c1991.
QB472.A1X234 1991

[B]Basic Science Seminar on Development of
Superconducting Radiation Detectors (43rd : 1995 : Tokyo,
Japan)
Dai 43-kai Kiso Kagaku Semin¯a "Ch¯o Dend¯o
H¯oshasen Kenshutsuki no Kaihatsu" ronbunsh¯u : 1995-nen
11-gatsu 20-nichi, Nihon Genshiryoku Kenky¯ujo, T¯oky¯o /
Ry¯oshi Keisoku Kenky¯u Gur¯upu.
Ibaraki-ken T¯okai-mura : Nihon Genshiryoku
Kenky¯ujo, 1996.
MLCMJ 98/521 (T)

[B]Beha, Hansjörg, 1951-
Digitale Speicherzellen mit Josephson-Kontakten =
Digital memory cells with Josephson junctions / Hansjörg
Beha.
Berlin : VDE-Verlag, 1981.
TK7868.L6B43 1981

[B]Bhasin, Kul B. , Vernon O. Heinen,
Superconductivity applications for infrared and microwave devices : 19-20 April 1990,
Orlando, Florida / chairs/editors ; sponsored by SPIE--the International Society for
Optical Engineering ;
cooperating organization, CREOL/University of Central Florida.
Bellingham, Wash., USA : The Society, c1990.
TK7872.T55S86 1990

[B]Buhrman, Robert A.
Superconductive devices and circuits : 25-27
January 1994, Los Angeles, California / Robert A. Buhrman ...
[et al.], chairs/editors ; sponsored and published by
SPIE--the International Society for Optical Engineering.
Bellingham, Wash. : SPIE, c1994.

TK7872.S8S795 1994

[B]Buhrman, Robert A.
Superconductive devices and circuits : 25-27
January 1994, Los Angeles, California / Robert A. Buhrman ...
[et al.], chairs/editors ; sponsored and published by
SPIE--the International Society for Optical Engineering.
Bellingham, Wash. : SPIE, c1994.
TK7872.S8S795 1994

[B]Chiara, Alessandro di, Maurizio Russo
Workshop on Josephson Devices (3rd : 1991 :
Capri, Italy)
Tunneling phenomena in high and low Tc
superconductors : proceedings of the Third Workshop on
Josephson Devices, Capri, Italy, 1-4 October 1991 / editors,
Alessandro di Chiara, Maurizio Russo.
Singapore ; River Edge, NJ : World Scientific, c1993.
QC610.9.W66 1991

[B]Costabile, Giovanni
Nonlinear superconductive electronics and
Josephson devices / edited by Giovanni Costabile ... [et al.].
New York : Plenum Press, c1991.
TK7872.S8N65 1991

[B]Crabtree, George W; Nelson, David R.; Vortex physics in high-temperature superconductors; Physics Today.v. 50 Apr. '97 p. 38-45.
The discovery of high-temperature superconductors has encouraged dramatic growth in the understanding of the physics of quantized vortex lines, creating new horizons in fundamental science and potential commercial applications. Vortices in superconductors offer a highly accessible example of flexible one-dimensional objects interacting through a simple potential in the presence of controlled disorder. In addition, technology has embraced the potential of high-temperature superconductors, with over 15 companies actively involved in developing products ranging from high-current bulk wires and tapes to thin film devices.

[B]Deutscher, Guy.
Superconductivity and cryogenics / by Guy Deutscher.
Jerusalem : Prime Minister's Office, National
Council for Research and Development, 1976.
TK454.4.S93D48

[B]E. Goto, K.F. Loe
RIKEN Symposia on Josephson Electronics (6th :
1989 : Tokyo, Japan)

Issues in Josephson supercomputer design /
editors, E. Goto, K.F. Loe.
Singapore ; Teaneck, NJ : World Scientific, c1991.
TK7895.P3I84 1991

[B]Goto, Eiichi, Takashi Soma, Loe Kia Fock
Fluxoid Josephson computer technology :
proceedings of the 3rd, 4th, and 5th RIKEN-ERATO symposia :
proceedings of the 3rd, 18 March 1986, 4th, 19 March 1987,
and 5th, 15 March 1988 symposia, Tokyo, Japan / editors,
Eiichi Goto, Takashi Soma, Loe Kia Fock.
Singapore ; Teaneck, NJ, USA : World Scientific, c1988.
TK7895.P3R55 1989

[B]H. D. Hahlbohm, and H. Lübbig.
International Conference on Superconducting
Quantum Devices (1st : 1976 : Berlin, Germany)
SQUID, superconducting quantum interference
devices and their applications : proceedings of the
International Conference on Superconducting Quantum Devices,
Berlin (West), October 5-8, 1976 / editors, H. D. Hahlbohm, H. Lübbig.
Berlin ; New York : W. de Gruyter, 1977.
TK7872.S8I57 1976

[B]H. D. Hahlbohm, and H.Lübbig.
International Conference on Superconducting
Quantum Devices (2nd : 1980 : Berlin, Germany)
SQUID '80, superconducting quantum interference
devices and their applications : proceedings of the Second
International Conference on Superconducting Quantum Devices,
Berlin (West), May 6-9, 1980 / editors, H. D. Hahlbohm, H. Lübbig.
Berlin ; New York : W. de Gruyter, 1980.
TK7872.S8I57 1980

[B]H.D. Hahlbohm, and H.Lübbig.
International Conference on Superconducting
Quantum Devices (3rd : 1985 : Berlin, Germany)
SQUID '85, superconducting quantum interference
devices and their applications : proceedings of the Third
International Conference on Superconducting Quantum Devices,
Berlin (West), June 25-28, 1985 / editors, H.D. Hahlbohm, H. Lübbig.
Berlin ; New York : W. de Gruyter, 1985.
TK7872.S8I57 1985

[B]Hara, Ko.
High temperature superconducting electronics :
basis for materials and device structures / Ko Hara, editor.
Tokyo : Ohmsha ; Amsterdam ; New York : IOS

Press, c1993.
TK7872.S8H37 1993

[B]Hecht, Jeff; Getting warmer; New Scientist.v. 159 no2145 Aug. 1 '98 p. 4.
A team at IBM, Zurich, Switzerland, has developed a means of dramatically increasing the temperatures at which one particular compound will conduct electricity with zero resistance. Locquet and his colleagues found that compressing the atoms of a ceramic containing lanthanum, strontium, and copper oxide raised the temperature at which the material would superconduct from 25 K to 49 K. Conversely, increasing the atomic spacing resulted in a reduction of the temperature to 10 K. These findings suggest that superconductivity at temperatures near 200 K may be achievable, enabling the creation of superconductivity devices that do not require expensive cooling systems.

[B]Hioe, Willy
Quantum flux parametron : a single quantum flux
superconducting logic device / Willy Hioe and Eiichi Goto.
Singapore ; Teaneck, NJ : World Scientific, c1991.
TK7895.P3H56 1991

[B]Koch, H. , H. Lübbig
Single-electron tunneling and mesoscopic devices
: proceedings of the 4th international conference, SQUID '91
(sessions on SET and mesoscopic devices), Berlin, Fed. Rep.
of Germany, June 18-21, 1991 / H. Koch, H. Lübbig, eds.
Berlin ; New York : Springer-Verlag, c1992.
QC610.9.S62 1992

[B]Koch, H. , H. Lübbig
Superconducting devices and their applications :
proceedings of the 4th international conference SQUID '91
(sessions on superconducting devices), Berlin, Fed. Rep. of
Germany, June 18-21, 1991 / H. Koch, H. Lübbig, eds.
Berlin ; New York : Springer-Verlag, c1992.
TK7872.S8S792 1992

[B]Likharev, K. K. (Konstantin Konstantinovich)
Dynamics of Josephson junctions and circuits /
Konstantin K. Likharev.
New York : Gordon and Breach Science Publishers, c1986.
QC176.8.T8L55 1986

[B]Loe, K. F. (Kia Fock)
DC flux parametron : a new approach to Josephson
junction logic / K.F. Loe, E. Goto.
Singapore ; Philadelphia, PA, USA : World Scientific, c1986.
TK7895.P3L64 1986

[B]Miska, Kurt H.
Superconductor component industry : markets for new and old technologies / Kurt H. Miska, project analyst.
Norwalk, Conn., U.S.A. : Business Communications Co., [1988], c1987.
HD9696.S692M57 1988

[B]Misugi, Takahiko and Akihiro Shibatomi
Compound and Josephson high-speed devices / edited by Takahiko Misugi and Akihiro Shibatomi.
New York : Plenum Press, c1993.
TK7874.7.C66 1993

[B]Palmer, D.N.(ed.)
Superconductivity advances and applications, 1989 :presented at the Winter Annual Meeting of the American Society of Mechanical Engineers, San Francisco, California, December 10-15, 1989 / sponsored by the Superconductivity Technical Committee of the Advanced Energy Systems Division, ASME ; New York, N.Y. : ASME, c1989.
QP82.2.M3S86 1989

[B]Parmentier, R.D. , N.F. Pedersen.
Nonlinear superconducting devices and high-Tc materials : proceedings of the international conference, Capri, Italy, 8-13 October 1994 / editors, R.D. Parmentier, N.F. Pedersen.
Singapore ; River Edge, NJ : World Scientific, c1995.
TK7872.S8N64 1995

[B]Radio Corporation of America. Defense Electronic Products.
Search radar, superconductor devices, data communications, spacecraft communications, speech recognition; seventeen technical papers, by RCA scientists and engineers.
[Camden, N.J., c1967]
TK7880.R3

[B]Rajendra Singh, J. Narayan, David T. Shaw
Progress in high-temperature superconducting transistors and other devices : 4-5 October 1990, Santa Clara, California / Rajendra Singh, J. Narayan, David T. Shaw, chairs/editors ; sponsored and published by SPIE--the International Society for Optical Engineering.
Bellingham, Wash., USA : SPIE, c1991.
TK7871.9.P73 1991

[B]Robert Joynt & Marshall Onellion
High Tõc superconducting thin films, devices, and applications, Atlanta, GA, 1988 / editors, Giorgio Margaritondo, Robert Joynt & Marshall Onellion.
New York, NY : American Institute of Physics, 1989.
TK7872.T55H53 1989

[B]Russo, M. , G. Costabile
Workshop on Stimulated Nonlinear Effects in Josephson Devices (1988 : Capri, Italy)
Stimulated effects in Josephson devices : proceedings of the Workshop on Stimulated Nonlinear Effects in Josephson Devices, Capri, Italy, 27-30 September 1988 / editors, M. Russo, G. Costabile.
Singapore ; Teaneck, NJ : World Scientific, c1990.
TK7872.S8W67 1988

[B]Schooley, James F.
Preparation and use of superconductive fixed point devices, SRM 767 [by]J. F. Schooley, R. J. Soulen, Jr., and G. A. Evans, Jr.
[Washington]U.S. National Bureau of Standards; [for sale by the Supt. of Docs., U.S. Govt. Print. Off.] 1972.
QC100.U57 no. 260-44

[B]Singh, Rajendra, Martin Nisenoff, Davor Pavuna
Progress in high-temperature superconducting transistors and other devices : 12-13 September 1991, San Jose, California / Rajendra Singh, Martin Nisenoff, Davor Pavuna, chairs/editors ; sponsored and published by SPIE--the International Society for Optical Engineering.
Bellingham, Wash.: SPIE, c1992.
TK7871.9.P74 1992

[B]Superconducting devices & materials / compiled by Cryogenic Data Center, Thermophysical Properties Division, National Bureau of Standards.
Boulder, Colo. : NBS,

[B]Superconducting devices & materials / compiled by Cryogenic Data Center, Thermophysical Properties Division, National Bureau of Standards.
Boulder, Colo. : NBS,

[B]van Dover, R. Bruce, Cheng-Chung Chi (eds.)
High-Tc superconductivity : thin films and
devices : 16-17 March 1988, Newport Beach, California /, sponsored by SPIE--the International Society for Optical Engineering ; cooperating organization, the Metallurgical Society. Bellingham, Wash., USA : SPIE, c1988.
TK7872.T55H54 1988

[B]Weinstock, , Harold
SQUID sensors : fundamentals, fabrication, and
applications / edited by Harold Weinstock.
Dordrecht ; Boston : Kluwer Academic Publishers, c1996.
TK7872.S8S65 1996

[B]Zimmerman, James E., and Thomas M. Flynn
Applications of closed-cycle cryocoolers to small
superconducting devices : proceedings of a conference held at
the National Bureau of Standards, Boulder, Colorado, October
3-4, 1977 / edited by James E. Zimmerman and Thomas M. Flynn
sponsored by National Bureau of Standards and Office of
Naval Research.
Washington : U.S. Dept. of Commerce, National
Bureau of Standards : for sale by the Supt. of Docs., U.S.
Govt. Print. Off., 1978.
QC100.U57 no. 508; Alternative class.: TK7872.S8

Materials

[C]Abe, Yoshihiro
Superconducting glass-ceramics in Bi-Sr-Ca-Cu-O :
fabrication and its application / editor, Yoshihiro Abe.
Singapore ; River Edge, N.J. : World Scientific, c1997.
QC611.98.C47S87 1997

[C]Bashilov, V.A.
Kompoziëtšionnye sverkhprovodëiìashchie
materialy voloknistogo stroeniëiìa / [V.A. Bashilov ... et al.].
Moskva : "Metallurgiëiìa", 1986.
TN693.S9K65 1986

[C]Biavati, Bruce J.
Evidence for an energy gap in superconducting
zinc [by]Bruce J. Biavati.
[New York]1964.
QC176.8.E4B5

[C]Brown, B. S., H. C. Freyhardt, T. H. Blewitt.
International Discussion Meeting on Radiation
Effects on Superconductivity, Argonne, Ill., 1977.
Radiation effects on superconductivity :
proceedings of the International Discussion Meeting on
Radiation Effects on Superconductivity, Argonne, Illinois,
USA, 13-16 June 1977,
Amsterdam ; New York : North-Holland Pub. Co. ;
New York : sole distributors for the U.S.A. and Canada,
Elsevier North-Holland, 1978.
QC612.S8I56 1977

[C]Bruce van Dover, R., Cheng-Chung Chi
High-Tc superconductivity : thin films and
devices : 16-17 March 1988, Newport Beach, California /, chairs/editors ; sponsored
by SPIE--the International Society for Optical Engineering ;
cooperating organization, the Metallurgical Society.
Bellingham, Wash., USA : SPIE, c1988.
TK7872.T55H54 1988

[C]Butera, R. A; Waldeck, D. H.; The dependence of resistance on temperature for metals, semiconductors, and superconductors; Journal of Chemical Education.v. 74 Sept. '97 p. 1090-4.
An experiment is described in which the temperature dependence of a metal, a semiconductor, and a superconductor is measured.

[C]Cai, X. Y; Polyanskii, A; Li, Q.; Current-limiting mechanisms in individual filaments extracted from superconducting tapes; Nature.v. 392 no6679 Apr. 30 '98 p. 906-9.
The transport properties of individual filaments extracted from very-high critical-current density (Jc) multifilament semiconductor tapes were measured. The Jc for individual filaments attained values about 50 percent higher than the average value over the whole cross-section of the wire. All the filaments had the local characteristics of c-axis transport even though the current was injected to flow along the crystallographic a-b planes of the material.

[C]Canfield, Paul C; Gammel, Peter L; Bishop, David J.; New magnetic superconductors: a toy box for solid-state physicists. Physics Today.v. 51 no10 Oct. '98 p. 40-6.
The rare earth nickel borocarbide compounds have reawakened interest in the question of how superconductivity and magnetism coexist. This series initially attracted interest because its members are magnetic superconductors for most of the heavy rare earth elements, high-quality samples can be easily produced in single-crystal form, and the energy scales for superconductivity and antiferromagnetic order can be extensively varied. At this point, the abundance of physical effects shown by the rare earth nickel borocarbide compounds has surpassed initial expectations. The authors discuss the discovery of the compounds, their basic properties, their low-field properties, the effects of an applied magnetic field on the superconducting state, the flux-line lattice of the compounds, and future work in the field.

[C]Chemistry and Related Aspects of High Temperature Superconductors
(Studies of High Temperature Superconductors -Volume 25)
Anant Narlikar (Ed.)
1998. 278 pages. ISBN 1-56072-539-7. $93
The present volume forms the sequel to the two previous volumes, the Vol. 23 and Vol. 24, which focused on the synthesis and properties of the Hg-based high Tc family. The mercurocuprates prominently appear again in this volume, but this time in conjunction with other interesting high Tc systems such as Y-124, BSCCO etc. The focus of the volume is on the problems linked with the structural chemistry and related crystallography which are extensively discussed in terms of many new ideas and understanding by expert contributors coming from different parts of the globe.
Contents: Preface; Chapter 1: Classification of Superconducting Oxides as Interstitial Alloys (J. Hauck and K. Mika); Chapter 2: Reconciliation Between Structural Features and Descriptions of High Tc Superconductors (Fujio Izumi); Chapter 3: Crystal Structures and Crystal Chemistry of Bi-Containing Compounds in the Bi-Sr-Ca-Cu-O System, A Review (Winnie Wong-Ng); Chapter 4: Studies on Preparation and

Substitution of $YBa_2Cu_4O_8$ (J. Valo and M. Leskela); Chapter 5: Crystal Chemistry of the Mercurocuprates (Graeme B. Peacock, Wuzong Zhou and Peter P. Edwards); Chapter 6: On the Synthesis and Structure of $HgBa_2Ca_{n-1}Cu_nO_{2n+2+\delta}$ Superconductors (Sergio M. Loureiro, Jean-Jacques Capponi, Eugene V. Antipov and Massimo Marezio); Chapter 7: Mercury Nonstoichiometry and Copper Valence in Bulk Hg-1201 (Giorgio A. Costa and Elena Kaiser)

[C]Chi, Cheng-Chung (John) , R. Bruce van Dover (eds.)
High Tc superconductivity, thin films and
applications : 20-21 March 1990, San Diego, California /
sponsored by SPIE--the International Society for Optical
Engineering, in cooperation with the Society of Vacuum Coaters.
Bellingham, Wash., USA : SPIE, c1990.
TK7872.T55H52 1990

[C]Choy, Jin Ho; Kwon, Soon Jae; Park, Gyeong Su; High-Tc superconductors in the two-dimensional limit: ((Py-CnH2n+1)2HgI4)-Bi2Sr2Cam-1CumOy (m = 1 and 2); Science.v. 280 no5369 June 5 '98 p. 1589-92.
The free modulation of interlayer distance in a layered high-transition temperature (high-Tc) superconductor is of crucial importance not only for the study of the superconducting mechanism but also for the practical application of high-Tc superconducting materials. Two-dimensional (2D) superconductors were achieved by intercalating a long-chain organic compound into bismuth-based high-Tc cuprates.

[C]Cogordan, J.A. et al. ...
Winter Meeting on Low Temperature Physics (11th :
1990 : Cocoyoc, Mexico)
Ceramic superconductors : proceedings of the XI
Winter Meeting on Low Temperature Physics, 14-17 January
1990, Cocoyoc, Morelos, Mexico / editors,
Singapore ; Teaneck, NJ : World Scientific, c1991.
QC611.98.C47W56 1990

[C]Collings, E. W.
A sourcebook of titanium alloy superconductivity / E.W. Collings.
New York : Plenum, c1983.
TN693.T5C64 1983

[C]Collings, E. W.
Applied superconductivity, metallurgy, and
physics of titanium alloys / E.W. Collings.
New York : Plenum Press, c1986.
TN693.T5C625 1986

[C]Conductor Developments of High Temperature Superconductors
(Volume 21 - Studies of High Temperature Superconductors)
Anant Narlikar (Ed.)
1997. 292 pages. ISBN 1-56072-419-6. $110.
TEXTURED BSCCO SUPERCONDUCTORS OBTAINED VIA LASER INDUCED DIRECTIONAL SOLIDIFICATION (L.A. Angurel, Et al. Instituto de Ciencia de Materiales de Aragon (ICMA), CSIC-Univ. de Zaragoza, Centro Politecnico Superior de Ingenieros, Maria de Luna 3, E-50015 Zaragoza, SPAIN); THE SUPERCONDUCTING AND MICROSTRUCTURAL BEHAVIOUR OF YBa2 Cu3 Oy AND YBa2 Cu3 Oy + Y2 BaCuO; SUPERCONDUCTORS PREPARED BY THE MELT TEXTURED GROWTH PROCESS (J.A. Xia and P.R. Munroe School of Materials Science and Engineering, Univ. of NSW, Sydney, NSW 2052, AUSTRALIA.); DEVELOPMENT OF Bi-2212/Ag WIRES FOR MAGNET APPLICATIONS; (R. Wesche, A.M. Fuchs and B. Jakob, Centre de Recherches en Physique des Plasmas, Technologie de la Fusion, Association Euroatom - Confederation Suisse, Ecole Polytechnique Federale de Lausanne, CH-5232 Villigen, SWITZERLAND) ; A NOVEL PROCESS FOR QUICK SYNTHESIS OF YITRIUM BASED HTSC. Shu-En Hsu (National Taiwan Univ., Taipei, Taiwan, REPUBLIC OF CHINA); Jc PROPERTY AND MICROSTRUCTURE OF Bi2223 TAPES MADE USING Ag-Cu ALLOY - SHEATHS DOPED WITH Ti, Zr OR Hf (Y. Tanaka (a), M. Ishizuka (b), L.L. He(c,d), S. Horiuchi (d) and H. Maeda (a) (a) National Research Inst.for Metals, 1-2-1 Sengen, Tsukuba 305, JAPAN.(b) Sumitomo Heavy Industries Ltd., 63-30 Yuhigaoka, Hiratsuka 254, JAPAN. (c) Inst.of Metal Research, Academia Sinica, 72 Wenhua Road, Shenyang 110015, PEOPLES REPUBLIC OF CHINA) (d) National Inst.for Research in Inorganic Materials, I-2 Namiki, Tsukuba 305, JAPAN.); FABRICATION OF Bi-2212/Ag COMPOSITE TAPES AND COILS . H. Kumakura, H. Kitaguchi, K. Togano and H. Meada (National Research Inst.for Metals, 1-2-1 Sengen, Tsukuba 305, JAPAN.); CRITICAL CURRENTS IN SILVER-SHEATHED (Bi, Pb)2 Sr2 Ca2 Cu3 O10 TAPES; (a) Centre for Superconducting and Electronic Materials, Univ. of Wollongong, Wollongong, NSW 2500, AUSTRALIA. (b) Siemens AG, Zentrale Forschung und Entwicklung, D-91052. Erlangen, GERMANY (c) Atoministut der Osterreichischen Universitaten, A-1020 Wien, AUSTRIA.; HIGH CRITICAL CURRENT DENSITIES IN SILVER SHEATHED Bi-2223 TAPES (Luciano Martini, CISE SpA, P.O. Box 12081, I-20134 Milan, ITALY); INVESTIGATION ON CRITICAL CURRENT AND MICROSTRUCTURE OF HIGH Tc Y-Ba-Cu-O SUPERCONDUCTORS (A.Q. He, G.F. Zhou, G.W. Qiao and H.Q. Ye. Laboratory of Atomic Imaging of Solids, Inst.of Metal Research, Shenyang 110015, PEOPLES REPUBLIC OF CHINA) Subject Index

[C]Cyrot, M.
Introduction to superconductivity and high-Tc materials / Michel Cyrot, Davor Pavuna.
Singapore ; River Edge, N.J. : World Scientific, c1992.
QC611.92.C97 1992

[C]Daugherty, Debra; Superconductors in a twist; New Scientist.v. 157 no2120 Feb. 7 '98 p. 32-5.
Scientists are now working to resolve the conflict between superconductivity and self-magnetism that has condemned high-temperature superconductors to underachievement. In these materials, magnetic fields spoil superconductivity by forming thousands of microscopic swirling currents that cause great problems when they move about. By learning to control their motion, however, researchers are beginning to develop a peaceful coexistence between superconductivity and magnetism, enabling superconducting technology to finally realize its potential.

[C]de Gennes, P. G.
Superconductivity of metals and alloys / P. G. de
Gennes, Translated by P. A. Pincus.
Reading, MA : Perseus Books, 1999.

[C]Demler, Eugene; Zhang, Shou Cheng; Quantitative test of a microscopic mechanism of high-temperature superconductivity; Nature.v. 396 no6713 Dec. 24-31 '98 p. 733-5.
A microscopic mechanism for the condensation energy of high-transition-temperature superconductors is proposed. The antiferromagnetic exchange energy in the superconducting state is lowered relative to the normal state within this mechanism due to the appearance of a resonance in the superconducting state. The intensity of the resonant neutron-scattering peak observed previously in YBa2Cu3O7 during the transition to the superconducting state is in quantitative agreement with the condensation energy of these materials.

[C]Douglass, D. H.(ed.)
Rochester Conference on Superconductivity in d-
and f-Band Metals, 2d, 1976.
Superconductivity in d- and f-band metals :
[proceedings of the] Second Rochester Conference [on
Superconductivity in d- and f-Band Metals held in Rochester,
New York, April 30-May 1, 1976]
New York : Plenum Press, c1976.
QC612.S8R58 1976

[C]Douglass, D. Jr., and R. W. Schmitt
International Conference on the Science of
Superconductivity, Colgate University, 1963.
International Conference on the Science of
Superconductivity; [proceedings. Edited by, assisted by G. E. Nichols.
New York? 1964]
QC612.S8I5 1963

[C]Eremets, M. I; Shimizu, K; Kobayashi, T. C.; Metallic CsI at pressures of up to 220 gigapascals; Science.v. 281 no5381 Aug. 28 '98 p. 1333-5.
Direct electrical transport measurements in a diamond anvil cell provide evidence for the metallization of cesium iodide (Csl) at a pressure of 115 gigapascals. A drop in the temperature dependence of the resistance was found at pressures above 180 gigapascals, indicating that the Csl was superconductive. The superconductivity changed under the influence of a magnetic field to a lower critical temperature and disappeared above 0.3 tesla. The highest critical temperature at which superconductivity was observed was 2 kelvin, and the critical temperature decreased with increasing pressure.

[C]Eskildsen, M. R; Harada, K; Gammel, P. L.; Intertwined symmetry of the magnetic modulation and the flux-line lattice in the superconducting state of TmNi2B2C; Nature.v. 393 no6682 May 21 '98 p. 242-5.
The flux-line lattice and magnetic order in the superconductor TmNi2B2C (Tm:1221) were investigated. Simultaneous small-angle neutron-scattering studies were augmented with extensive characterization by transport and magnetization. The structure of the magnetic modulation and the symmetry of the flux-line lattice were found to be intimately coupled, affording a complex phase diagram.

[C]Evetts, J.E.
Concise encyclopedia of magnetic &
superconducting materials / editor, J.E. Evetts.
Oxford ; New York : Pergamon Press, 1992.
QC764.52.C66 1992

[C]Falge, Raymond L.
Measurement of various properties of titanium in
the superconducting state, by Raymond L. Falge.
Washington, Catholic University of America Press,
1966.
QC612.S8F3

[C]Faulques, Eric
Spectroscopy of superconducting materials / Eric
Faulques, editor.
Washington, DC : American Chemical Society, 1999.
QC611.97.S64S65 1999

[C]Fischer, Ø., and M.B. Maple with contributions by S.
Alterovitz ... [et al.].
Superconductivity in ternary compounds
Berlin ; New York : Springer-Verlag, 1982-
QC612.S8S83 1982

[C]Fisk, Zachary; Pines, David; The ghost of magnetism; Nature.v. 394 no6688 July 2 '98 p. 22-3.
In this issue, the authors report the possible existence of a magnetic pairing mechanism in superconducting materials. The researchers studied 2 heavy-fermion superconductors in which a magnetically ordered state of cerium 4f-local moments is in competition with a heavy-fermion state that has all of these moments compensated by conduction electrons. In these materials, pressure increases the conduction-electron/4f-moment coupling, favoring the heavy-fermion state; however, superconductivity emerges in between low-temperature magnetic order and heavy-fermion behavior due, according to the researchers, to magnetically mediated pairing.

[C]Gennes, Pierre-Gilles de.
Superconductivity of metals and alloys [by] P.G. de Gennes. Translated by P.A. Pincus.
New York, W.A. Benjamin, 1966.
QC612.S8G4

[C]Gennes, Pierre-Gilles de.
Superconductivity of metals and alloys / P.G. de Gennes ; translated by P.A. Pincus.
Redwood City, Calif. : Addison-Wesley, c1989.
QC611.92.G46 1989

[C]Ginzburg, V.L. and D.A. Kirzhniëtìs
Problema vysoko-temperaturnoæi sverkhprovodimosti. English.
High-temperature superconductivity / translated from Russian by A.K. Agyei ; translation edited by Joseph L. Birman.
New York : Consultants Bureau, c1982.
QC612.S8P7613 1982

[C]Glattli, D.C., M. Sanquer, J. Trân Thanh Vân.
Moriond Workshop (14th : 1994 : Villars-sur-Ollon, Switzerland)
Coulomb and interference effects in small electronic structures : proceedings of the XXIXth Rencontre de Moriond, series: Moriond condensed matter physics, Villars sur Ollon, Switzerland, January 22-29, 1994 / edited by D.C. Glattli, M. Sanquer, J. Trân Thanh Vân.
Gif-sur-Yvette, France : Editions Frontieres, c1994.
QC176.8.E4M62 1994

[C]Goldman, Allen M; Markovic, Nina; Superconductor-insulator transitions in the two-dimensional limit; Physics Today.v. 51 no11 Nov. '98 p. 39-44.
The writer discusses topics, including disordered thin films, aspects of superconductivity,

quantum phase transitions, the dirty-boson model, and the experimental situation.

[C]Gorter, C. J. (Cornelis Jacobus), 1907-
Lectures on magnetism and superconductivity, by
C. J. Gorter. Notes by S. Doraiswamy [and others].
Bombay, Tata Institute of Fundamental Research,
1963 [cover 1965]
QC753.G58

[C]Gorzkowski, W. et al.
European Conference on High-Tc Thin Films and
Single Crystals (1989 : Ustroân, Poland)
Proceedings of the European Conference on High-Tc
Thin Films and Single Crystals Sept. 30--Oct. 4, 1989,
Ustrón, Poland
Singapore ; Teaneck, NJ : World Scientific, c1990.
QC176.84.R3E97 1989

[C]H.-U. Habermeier, E. Kaldis, and J.Schoenes.
Symposium A on High TC Superconductor Materials
(1990 : Strasbourg, France)
High TC superconductor materials : proceedings of
Symposium A on High TC Superconductor Materials of the 1990
E-MRS spring conference, Strasbourg, France, 29 May-1 June
1990 / edited by H.-U. Habermeier, E. Kaldis, and J. Schoenes.
Amsterdam ; New York : North-Holland ; New York,
N.Y., U.S.A. : Sole distributors for the USA and Canada,
Elsevier Science Pub. Co., 1990-
TK7872.S8S95 1990

[C]Heiras, J.L. , L.E. Sansores, A.A. Valladares.
Winter Meeting on Low Temperature Physics (12th :
1991 : Morelos, México)
Superconducting ceramics : XII Winter Meeting on
Low Temperature Physics, Vista Hermosa, Morelos, México,
13-16 January, 1991
Singapore ; River Edge, N.J. : World Scientific, c1991.
QC611.98.C47W56 1991

[C]Hemley, Russell J.; Superconductivity in a grain of salt; Science.v. 281 no5381 Aug. 28 '98 p. 1296-7.
In this issue, Eremets and colleagues from Osaka University report that the ionic solid CsI is a metal and a superconductor when compressed above 200 GPa (2 megabars). The researchers pressed CsI into the metallic state and immediately measured the temperature and pressure dependence of the electrical resistance of the sample. They initially offer

direct evidence for metallization at 115 GPa, but upon further increase in pressure they noted a characteristic drop in resistance at 2 K near 180 GPa.

[C]Hemley, Russell J; Ashcroft, Neil W.; The revealing role of pressure in the condensed matter sciences; Physics Today.v. 51 no8 Aug. '98 pt1 p. 26-32.
The authors examine how high-pressure experiments have been used to induce insulator-to-metal transitions in ionic salts and rare-gas solids, elucidate the physics of hydrogen and water at high pressures, form new materials, transform simple alkali metals and alkaline earth metals into transition metals, and synthesize new superconductors and test superconductivity theory.

[C]Hg-Based High Tc Superconductors (Volume 23-Part I. Studies of High Temperature superconductors)
Anant Narlikar (Ed.)
1997. 287 pages. ISBN 1-56072-472-2. $95.
The "Studies" present the work on Hg-based high Tc cuprates in two parts; this volume, Vol. 23, forming the first part. It comprises 7 chapters devoted to the challenging issues of their synthesis, structural chemistry, microstructures, doping effects, the acoustic, magnetic, thermal, electrical and various other related properties of frontal importance. All the contributors are researchers from the established groups engaged in the studies of Hg-based cuprate systems.
Contents: Chapter 1- A Review of the Synthesis and Properties of Hg-Containing Superconductors, Focused on Bulk Materials and Thin Films (Ingrid Bryntse); Chapter 2- Single Crystals of Mercury Based Cuprates: Growth, Structure and Physical Properties (A. Bertinotti, D. Colson, J.F. Marucco, V.Viallet, G. Le Bras, L. Fruchter, C. Marcenat, A. Carrington, J. Hammann); Chapter 3- On Structural and Transport Properties of Hg-Based High Tc Superconductors (J.B. Mandal, B. Bandyopadhyay, P. Mandal, P. Chouhury, A.N. Das and B. Ghosh); Chapter 4- Acoustic Attenuation Studies on Flux Dynamics, Structure Instability and Carriers Pairing in Hg-Based High Tc Cuprates (Y.N. Wang, W.Tian, Q.M. Zhang, Y.N. Huang, J.S. Zhu and H.M. Shen); Chapter 5- Superconducting Hg-1223 Films Obtained by a Sol-Gel Process (Shimon Reich); Chapter 6- Hg-Based Homologous Series Superconductors, Hg-12(n-1)n and (Hg,T1)-22(n-1)n (S. Adachi, A Tokiwa-Yamamoto, A. Fukuoka, R. Usami, T. Tatsuki, Y. Moriwaki, K. Tanabe); Chapter 7- The Synthesis, Structure and Superconductivity of Mercury-Based Strontium Cuprates (Qian Yitai, Tang Kaibin, Zhang Yuheng)

[C]Hg-Based High Tc Superconductors
(Volume 24-Part II. Studies of High Temperature Superconductors)
Anant Narlikar (Ed.)
1997. 244 pages. ISBN 1-56072-524-9. $93.
This, the 24th volume of "Studies" is the continuation of Vol. 23 and forms the part-II of the advances in research and applications of Hg-based superconductors. The volume carries 7 chapters written by some of the pioneers in this field, from 8 different countries, keeping up with the international character of the book series.

Chapter 1: The Synthesis of Mercury-Based Copper Oxide Superconductors and Their Characteristics (C.C. Lamm, H.M. Shao); Chapter 2: X-Ray Single Crystal Structure Analysis of $HgBa_2$ Ca_{n-1} Cu_n $O_{2n+2+\delta}$ (n=1, 5) Homologous Series (H. Schwer and J. Karpinski); Chapter 3: Hg-Based Superconducting Filaments (Tomoko Goto); Chapter 4: Hg-Ba-Ca-Cu-O High Tc Thin Films and Superconducting Quantum Interference Devices (Neeraj Khare, A.K. Gupta, Sangeeta Khare and H.K. Singh); Chapter 5: Synthesis and Electron Microscopic Investigation of Hg and T1/Pb Doped Hg HTSC Phases in Bulk and Thin Film Forms (A.K. Srivastava, H.K. Singh and O.N. Srivastava); Chapter 6: High Pressure Synthesis and Properties of $HgBa_2$ Ca_{n-1} Cu_n $O_{2n+2+\delta}$, Y_2 Ba_4 Cu_{6+n} O_{14+n}, $Sr_{1-x}Ca_x$ CuO_2 and Sr_{0-73} CuO_2 Crystals (J. Karpinski, H. Schwer, R. Molinski, G.I. Meager, K. Conder, E. Kopnin, J. Lohle, C. Rossel, D. Zech, J. Hofer, A Wisniewski, R. Puzniak); Chapter 7: High Pressure Measurements on Mercury Cuprates (Manuel Nunez-Regueiro, Carolos Acha)

[C]High temperature superconducting materials : the
current situation / [by the editors at Japan Technical
Information Service].
Metals Park, Ohio : ASM International, c1987.
QC611.98.H54H543 1987

[C]High Temperature Superconductity - Current Results and Novel Mechanisms
K.P. Sinha and S.L. Kakani (Eds.)
1995. 312 pages. ISBN 1-56072-133-2. $110.
Superconductivity. One of the most exciting developments in science in recent years is the discovery of high-temperature superconductivity. This significant discovery has posed the two new problems of making high temperature superconducting materials available to technology at liquid nitrogen or even high temperatures on one hand and of exploring the possible mechanism of high-temperature superconductivity on the other. This outstanding book aims at summarizing results in this fast-moving realm of research.

[C]Hsieh, Shih-yung,
Quasiparticle recombination and diffusion in
superconducting aluminum films. [1970?]
QC176.8.E4H75

[C]International Conference on Materials and
Mechanisms of Superconductivity. High Superconductors.
Proceedings of the International Conference on
Materials and Mechanisms of Superconductivity,
Temperature Superconductors.
Amsterdam, The Netherlands : North Holland,
QC611.98.H54I57

[C]Ishida, K; Mukuda, H; Kitaoka, Y.; Spin-triplet superconductivity in Sr2RuO4 identified by 17O knight shift; Nature.v. 396 no6712 Dec. 17 '98 p. 658-60.
Evidence that Cooper electron pairs in the layered oxide superconductor Sr2RuO4 can exist in a spin-triplet state is reported. Knight shift, as determined by 17O nuclear magnetic resonance, was used to determine the spin susceptibility of the Cooper pairs. There was no change in spin susceptibility on passing through the superconducting transition temperature, which demonstrates that Sr2RuO4 is a spin-triplet superconductor.

[C]Kaldis, E.
Materials and crystallographic aspects of
HTc-superconductivity
Dordrecht ; Boston : Kluwer Academic Publishers, c1994.
QC611.98.H54M38 1994

[C]Kastner, M. A; Birgeneau, R. J; Shirane, G.; Magnetic, transport, and optical properties of monolayer copper oxides; Reviews of Modern Physics.v. 70 no3 July '98 p. 897-928.
The authors reviewed the results of neutron, optical, transport, and magnetization measurements made on large single crystals of copper oxides containing CuO2 layers. The purpose was to characterize the magnetic charge and charge excitations in these materials and to evaluate the importance of doping, in order to elucidate the mechanism of high temperature superconductivity.

[C]Kazakov, S. M; Chaillout, C; Bordet, P.; Discovery of a second family of bismuth-oxide-based superconductors; Nature.v. 390 Nov. 13 '97 p. 148-50.
The synthesis of a second family of superconducting bismuth oxides based on SrBiO3 (1) is reported. The synthesis of (1) entailed the preparation of Sr2Bi2O5 (2) through the annealing of an appropriate mixture of SrCO3 and Bi2O3 in air at 850[degree]C for 50 h, followed by the treatment of (2) at 800[degree]C for 35 h under high oxygen pressure. Partial substitution of potassium or rubidium for strontium was found to induce superconductivity with transition temperatures of [similar] 12 K for Sr1-xKxBiO3 (x = 0.45-0.6) and [similar] 13 K for Sr0.5Rb0.5BiO3.

[C]Kitazawa, Koichi, and Kyoji Tachikawa.
MRS International Meeting on Advanced Materials
(1st : 1988 : Tokyo, Japan)
Superconductivity : May 31-June 3, 1988, Sunshine
City, Ikebukuro, Tokyo, Japan
Pittsburgh, Pa. : Materials Research Society, c1989.
TA401.3.M77 1988 vol. 6; Alternative class.:
QC611.9

[C]Kockerling, Martin; Johrendt, Dirk; Finckh, E. Wolfgang; Superconductivity in Nb21S8, a phase with metal cluster chains; Journal of the American Chemical Society.v.

120 no47 Dec. 2 '98 p. 12297-302.
Phase pure samples of Nb21S8 are obtained by chemical transport and molten flux reactions in sealed niobium containers at 850-950 [degree]C. In the temperature range from 5 to 290 K the electrical conductivity is found to be moderate metallic with a specific resistivity of 3.90 mQ cm at 273 K. Magnetic susceptibility measurements give weak, almost temperature independent paramagnetism above [similar] 40 K. These metallic properties are compared with the structure of Nb21S8, which contains linear single and double chains of fused body centered niobium cubes, separated by S and additional Nb atoms.

[C]Kolodziejczyk, Andrzej.
Magnetyzm i nadprzewodnictwo Y_b9_sCo_b7_s.
English
Magnetism and superconductivity of Y_b9_sCo_b7_s
a contribution to the problems of 3d-electron magnetism in metals and their compounds and to the problems of 3d-electron magnetism in metals and their compounds and to the problem of coexistence of ferromagnetism and superconductivity / Andrzej Kolodziejczyk.
Crakow : Stanislaw Staszic Academy of Mining and Metallurgy, 1986.

[C]Kovachev, V.
Energy dissipation in superconducting materials / V. Kovachev ; edited by D. Dew-Hughes.
Oxford : Clarendon Press ; New York : Oxford University Press, 1991.
QC611.98.T87K69 1990

[C]Kuzmany, H. , M. Mehring,J. Fink
Electronic properties of high-Tc superconductors
the normal and the superconducting state of high-Tc materials : proceedings of the international winter school, Kirchberg, Tyrol, March 7-14, 1992 / H. Kuzmany, M. Mehring, J. Fink, eds.
Berlin ; New York : Springer, c1993.
QC611.98.H54E35 1993

[C]Luhman, Thomas and David Dew-Hughes
Metallurgy of superconducting materials / edited by Thomas Luhman and David Dew-Hughes.
New York : Academic Press, 1979.
TA403.T74 vol. 14; Alternative class.: TN693.S9

[C]Luke, G. M; Fudamoto, Y; Kojima, K. M.; Time-reversal symmetry-breaking superconductivity in Sr2RuO4; Nature.v. 394 no6693 Aug. 6 '98 p. 558-61.

The breaking of time-reversal symmetry in a superconductor is reported. Muon spin-relaxation measurements on Sr2RuO4 showed the spontaneous appearance of a magnetic field below the transition temperature, which suggests that the superconducting state in this material is marked by TRS breaking. These findings, together with other symmetry considerations, indicate that superconductivity in Sr2RuO4 is of "p-wave" (odd-parity) type, analogous to superfluid 3He.

[C]Maple, M.B., and Ø. Fischer ; with contributions by H.F. Braun
Superconductivity in ternary compounds II :
superconductivity and magnetism
Berlin ; New York : Springer-Verlag, 1982.
QC612.S8S833 1982

[C]Mathur, N. D; Grosche, F. M; Julian, S. R.; Magnetically mediated superconductivity in heavy fermion compounds; Nature.v. 394 no6688 July 2 '98 p. 39-43.
A study was carried out to determine whether it is possible to tune the nature of charge carrier interactions such that magnetic coupling demonstrably dominates the more conventional nonmagnetic channels of communication. Evidence that magnetically mediated form of superconductivity exists in some heavy fermion compounds, such as CePd2Si2 and CeIn3, is presented. This kind of superconductivity is normally only viable very close to the critical lattice density at which long-range magnetic order is suppressed and in specimens of extremely high purity. A magnetic-interaction model that provides a natural description of the temperature-density phase diagrams observed in CePd2Si2 and CeIn3 is described.

[C]Matsubara, T., and A. Kotani
Taniguchi International Symposium on the Theory
of Condensed Matter (6th : 1983 : Kashikojima, Japan)
Superconductivity in magnetic and exotic
materials : proceedings of the Sixth Taniguchi International
Symposium, Kashikojima, Japan, November 14-18, 1983
Berlin ; New York : Springer, c1984.
QC612.S8T36 1983

[C]Mayaffre, H; Auban Senzier, P; Nardone, M.; Absence of a spin gap in the superconducting ladder compound Sr2Ca12Cu24O41; Science.v. 279 Jan. 16 '98 p. 345-8.
Transport and copper-63 nuclear magnetic resonance measurements of the Knight shift and relaxation time T1 performed on the two-leg spin ladders of Sr2Ca12Cu24O41 single crystals as a function of pressure show a collapse of the gap in ladder spin excitations when superconductivity is stabilized at 31 kilobars.

[C]McKenzie, Ross H.; Similarities between organic and cuprate superconductors; Science.v. 278 Oct. 31 '97 p. 820-1.

When superconductivity was identified in organic solids based on the bis(ethylenedithio)-tetrathiafulvalene molecule, it was uncertain whether these peculiar materials were related to the equally unusual high-temperature cuprate superconductors. The author discusses recent research demonstrating that the organics exhibit some of the same interesting physics as the cuprates, including unconventional metallic properties.

[C]Mead, Carver A.; Collective electrodynamics I; Proceedings of the National Academy of Sciences of the United States of America.v. 94 June 10 '97 p. 6013-18.
The derivation of standard results of electromagnetic theory from the direct interaction of macroscopic quantum systems is presented. These results are obtained using only the assumptions of the Einstein-deBroglie relations, the discrete nature of charge, the Green's function for the vector potential, and the continuity of the wave function. Correspondence limits based on classical mechanics were shown to be inappropriate.
[C]Microstructural Studies of High Tc Superconductors and more on Quaternary Borocarbides
Studies of High Temperature Superconductors - Volume 28
(Advances in Research and Applications)
Anant Narlikar (Ed.) (National Physical Laboratory, New Delhi)
1999. 287 pages. ISBN 1-56072-685-7. $93.
Contents: Chapter 1: Microstructure of Melt-Grown $REBa_2Cu_3O_{7-x}$ Superconductors (Favel Diko, Institute of Experimental Physics, Slovak Academy of Sciences, Slovakia); Chapter 2: Defects and Microstructural Engineering in Melt Textured RE-123 Superconductors (F. Sandiumenge, Institut de Ciencia de Materials de Barcelona, Spain and J. Rabier Laboratoire de Metallurgie Physique, France); Chapter 3: Refinement of Y_2BaCuO_5 and Distribution of Microstructural Inhomogeneities in Melt-Processed YBCO Superconductors (Chan-Joong Kim, Korea Atomic Energy Research Institute); Chapter 4: Real Domain Structure Originating in (110) Mechanic Twinning In YBCO (Alicia Rosova, Institute of Electrical Engineering, Slovak Academy of Sciences, Slovakia); Chapter 5: Microstructure and Superconducting Characteristics of Hg-Pb-Ba-Ca-Cu-O (I. Sargankova, P. Diko, Slovak Academy of Sciences, W. Konig, M. Mair, G. Gritzner, Johannes Kepler Universitat, M. Reissner, Technical University of Vienna); Chapter 6: Microstructure Studies in Ramp Type High Tc Josephson Junctions (J. Gao, University of Hong Kong); Chapter 7: Transport in the Rare Earth - Nickel - Borocarbides (D.G. Naugle and K.D.D. Rathanayaka, Texas A&M University and A.K. Bhatnager, School of Physics, University of Hyderabad, India); Chapter 8: Superconductivity and Magnetism Quaternary Borocarbides and Boronitrides (Gerfried Hilscher and Herwig Michor, Institut fur Experimentalphysik, Technische Universitat Wien)

[C]Moon, Francis C.
Mechanics of superconducting structures :
presented at the winter annual meeting of the American
Society of Mechanical Engineers, Chicago, Illinois, November
16-21, 1980 / sponsored by the Applied Mechanics Division,

ASME ; edited by Francis C. Moon.
New York, N.Y. : ASME, c1980.
TK7872.S8M43

[C]Mori, S; Chen, C. H; Cheong, S. W.; Pairing of charge-ordered stripes in (La,Ca)MnO3; Nature.v. 392 no6675 Apr. 2 '98 p. 473-6.
A novel pattern of charge localization in the charge-ordered phase of the manganese oxide La1-xCaxMnO3 (x [greater or equal] 0.5) is reported. The pattern takes the form of very stable pairs of Mn3+O6 stripes, with associated large lattice contractions that are separated periodically by stripes of non-distorted Mn4+O6 octahedra. These periodicities, which have integer values 2-5 times the lattice parameter of the orthorhombic unit cell, correspond to the commensurate carrier concentrations.

[C]Moskalenko, V. A. (Vsevolod Anatol'evich)
Nizkotemperaturnye svoæistva metallov s osobennostëĭami zonnogo spektra / V.A. Moskalenko, L.Z. Kon, M.E. Palistrant ; pod redakëtsieæi A.A. Goluba.
Kishinev : "Shtiinëtsa", 1989.
TK7872.S8M67 1989

[C]Musso, J. , J.-R. Gavarri
Conference on the Active Superconducting Composites (1st : 1996 : Université Toulon-Var)
CCAS1 : actes du premier Colloque sur les composites actifs supraconducteurs = proceedings of the First Conference on the Active Superconducting Composites, Université Toulon-Var, Toulon-La Garde, 11 et 12 Septembre 1996 / editeurs, J. Musso, J.-R. Gavarri.
Les Ulis, France : EDP Sciences, c1998.
TA418.9.C6C6396 1996

[C]Nair, K.M., and E.A. Giess.
Superconductivity and ceramic superconductors /
Westerville, Ohio : American Ceramic Society, c1990.
QC611.9.S85 1990

[C]Nair, K.M.,
Superconductivity and ceramic superconductors II
Westerville, Ohio : American Ceramic Society, c1991.
QC611.9.S853 1991

[C]Nakajima, S.
The science of superconductivity and new materials : proceedings of the Tokai University international workshop, Tokyo, Japan, 14-16 Nov. 1988
Singapore ; Teaneck, N.J. : World Scientific, c1989.

QC611.9.S37 1989

[C]Narlikar, A. V., 1940-
Superconductivity and superconducting materials /
A.V. Narlikar & S.N. Ekbote.
New Delhi : South Asian Publishers, c1983.
QC612.S8N36 1983

[C]Nesterenko, V.F., A.A. Schtertser
International Seminar on High Energy Working of
Rapidly Solidified Materials (1988 : Novosibirsk,
R.S.F.S.R.)
High energy working of rapidly solidified and
high temperature superconducting materials : proceedings of
the international seminar, Novosibirsk, October 10-14, 1988 /
edited by V.F. Nesterenko, A.A. Schtertser.
Novosibirsk : [SKB gidroimpul'snoæi tekhniki], 1989.
TS247.I6 1988

[C]Nichols, Roy and James A. Ionson
Sensing, discrimination, and signal processing
and superconducting materials and instrumentation : 12-14
January 1988, Los Angeles, California : part of the 1988
Innovative Science and Technology Symposium, James A. Ionson,
symposium chair / Roy Nichols, James A. Ionson,
chairs/editors ; sponsored by SPIE--the International Society
for Optical Engineering.
Bellingham, Wash., USA : The Society, c1988.
TA1505.S45 1988

[C]Noakes, David Ronald, 1954-
Crystalline electric field effects in rare earth
based magnetic and superconducting compounds [microform]/ by
David Ronald Noakes. 1983.
Microfilm 84/2039 (Q)

[C]Pace, S. and M. Acquarone.
Italian National School on Condensed Matter
Physics (24th : 1989 : Bra, Italy)
Superconductivity : proceedings of the XXIV
Italian National School on Condensed Matter Physics, Bra,
Italy, 18-28 September 1989 / editors,
Singapore ; River Edge, NJ : World Scientific, c1991.
QC611.9.I63 1989

[C]Palmer, David N.
Advances in superconducting materials and electronics technologies : presented at the Winter Annual Meeting of the American Society of Mechanical Engineers, Dallas, Texas, November 25-30, 1990 / sponsored by the Advanced Energy Systems Division, ASME ; edited by David N. Palmer.
New York, N.Y. : The Society, c1990.
TK7872.S8A38 1990

[C]Pardo, F; de la Cruz, F; Gammel, P. L.; Observation of smectic and moving-Bragg-glass phases in flowing vortex lattices; Nature.v. 396 no6709 Nov. 26 '98 p. 348-50.
The results of magnetic decoration studies of flowing vortex lattices are reported. In the magnetic decoration technique used, the flux-line lattice (FLL) is visualized by evaporating [similar] 50 A magnetic particles onto the surface of a superconductor held below its transition temperature with a magnetic field applied. The results provide evidence for a transition, as a function of increasing flux density, from a layered FLL to a more well-ordered moving Bragg glass.

[C]Phillips, Philip; Wan, Yi; Martin, Ivar; Superconductivity in a two-dimensional electron gas; Nature.v. 395 no6699 Sept. 17 '98 p. 253-7.
A study was carried out to analyze the experiments that have found a new conducting phase in dilute 2-D electron gases in zero magnetic field. The conventional theory of metals precludes the existence of a metallic state at zero temperature in 2 dimensions. On the basis of the analysis and general theoretical grounds, it is argued that the new phase is in fact a superconductor with an inhomogeneous charge density.

[C]Physical and Material Properties of High Temperature Superconductors
S.K. Malik and S.S. Shah (Eds.)
1994. 711 pages. ISBN 1-56072-114-6. $170.
Superconductivity; Materials Science
Partial Contents: Chemistry and Superconductivity of O_{5+d} 1201 Thallium Cuprates; Phase Formation and Superconducting Properties of $LnBaSrCu_3O_7$ Compounds (V. Badri, U.V. Vardaraju and G.V. Subba Rao); Structure and Properties of Electron Superconductors; The Influence of Pr and Cm on the Superconducting Properties of High-Tc Oxides (L. Soderholm and C.W. Williams); Synthesis, Crystal Structure and Physical Properties of the $Pb_2Sr_2RCu_3O_{8+d}$ System (J.S. Xue, M. Reedyk and J.E. Greedan); Current Directions in the Architecture of High-Tc Superconducting Oxides - A Review; Characterization of Superconducting Fullerenes; Transport Properties of Y-Doped Bi- and Tl-Based Superconductors; On the Magnitude of Resistivity in High-Temperature Cuprate Superconductors; Chemical Doping and Charge Balance in High Temperature Superconductors; Hidden Aspects of the Valence and Superconductivity.

[C]Physical Characteristics and Critical Temperature of High Temperature Superconductors
M.M. Sushchinskiy
227 pages, 1991. (Vol. 195 - Proc. of the Lebedev Physics Inst.). $140. ISBN 1-56072-039-5.
Superconductivity; Solid State Physics; Materials Science Contents: Relationship of Critical Temperature with Physical Characteristics of Superconductors: Atomic Characteristics; Tc and the Number of Valent Electrons of an Atom; Correlation of Tc with Concentration of Valent Electrons; Atomic Volume; Atomic Mass in High-Temperature Superconductors; Examples of Other Correlations with Atomic Values; Electron Characteristics; State Density on Fermi Surface; Concentration of Conductivity Electrons; Relationship of Conductivity Electron and Valent; Electron Correlations; Mean Velocity of Electrons on Fermi Surface; Area of Fermi Surface; Fourier Components of Pseudopotential; Theoretical Analysis of Relationship of Pseudopotential to Superconductivity; Electron-Phonon Interaction; Electron-Phonon Interaction Constant; Position of Peaks in Phonon State Density; Anomalies in Phonon Dispersion Curves; Temperature Changes in Phonon Spectrum Shape; Frequency of Collisions Between Electrons and Phonons.

[C]Physical Properties of High Temperature Superconductors
Yu. I.Koptev (Ed.)
1993. 235 pages. ISBN 1-56072-099-9. $135.
Partial Contents: Magnetization and Critical Current in High-Tc Superconductors; Electric Transport Properties of $YBa_2Cu_3O_{7-d}$ Based, High-Tc Polycrystalline Materials in the Temperature Range 77-450 K; Electrical Properties and Peculiarities of Mixed State of $YBaCu_3O_y$; Anisotropy in the Thermopower of Superconducting $YBa_2Cu_3O_{7-d}$ Single Crystals in the Temperature Range 8-300 K; Optical Properties of Single Crystals of High-Tc Superconductors: Y-Ba-Cu-O and Ba-Sr-Ca-Cu-O; Electrical and Mechanical Effects and Micro-Deformation in High-Tc Superconductors.

[C]Pseudogap in High Temperature Superconductors
Studies of High Temperature Superconductors - Volume 27
Anant Narlikar (Ed.) (National Physical Laboratory, New Delhi)
1999. 286 pages. ISBN- 1-56072-684-9. $89.
The present volume is devoted to the normal state pseudogap discovered in high Tc cuprates, which is currently an area of great topical interest and still not fully understood. The articles, written by the renowned experts in the field, consolidate the experimental findings and present various theoretical models to explain the occurrence of the gap. Contents: Chapter 1: Analysis of Properties of High Tc Superconductors (J. Schmalian and K.H. Bennemann, Institute of Theoretical Physics, Freie Universitat Berlin); Chapter 2: Doping Dependence of the Pseudogap in High Temperature Superconductors: A Raman Study (J.C. Irwin, J.G. Naeini and X.K. Chen, Physics Dept, Simon Fraser University); Chapter 3: NMR Studies of the Normal State Pseudogap in High

Temperature Superconducting Cuprates (G.V.M. Williams, New Zealand Institute for Industrial Research); Chapter 4: Some Theoretical Models for the Pseudogap in HTSC (K.P. Sinha, Indian Institute of Science); Chapter 5: The Fluctuation - Induced Pseudogap in the Optical Conductivity of High Tc Superconductors (Andrei A. Varlamov, Moscow Institute of Steel and Alloys); Chapter 6: Pseudogaps and Magnetic Properties of the Two Dimensional t-J Model (A. Sherman, Institute of Physics, University of Tartu); Chapter 7: Charge Dynamics via the Blocking Layer and the Pseudogap of High Tc Superconductors (J. Halbrittter, Institut fur Materialforschung); Chapter 8: Superconducting Pairing and the Collective Magnetic Excitation in the Extended 2-Dimensional t-J Model (Oleg Sushkov, School of Physics, University of New South Wales)

[C]Quaternary Borocarbide Superconductors and Hg-Based High Tc Superconductors
Studies of High Temperature Superconductors -Volume 26
(Advances in Research and Applications)
Anant Narlikar (Ed)
1998. 279 pages. ISBN 1-56072-628-8. $97
Contents: Chapter 1: Discovery of Superconducting Quaternary Borocarbide system Y-Ni-B-C and its Impact on Superconductivity and its Interplay with Magnetism (R. Nagarajan and L.C. Gupta- Tata Institute of Fundamental Research); Chapter 2: The Interrelation Between Magnetism and Superconductivity in R-Ni-B-C (R=Rare-Earth) (I. Felner - Racah Institute of Physics, the Hebrew University); Chapter 3: Dependence of Superconductivity and Magnetism on Materials Parameters in Quaternary Borocarbides (H. Schmidt and H.F. Braun - Physikalisches Institut, Universitat Bayreuth, Germany); Chapter 4: Properties of R-Ni-B-C (R=Y, Er) Superconducting Thin Films (A. Androne, C. Aruta, F. Fontana, M. Iavarone, M.L. Russo and R. Vaglio - INFM-Universita di Napoli and G. W. Crabtree and Y. De Wilde - Science and Technology Centre for Superconductivity, Argonne National Laboratory); Chapter 5; Synthesis and Characterization of the Superconducting Quaternary Intermetallic Compound Y-Ni-B-C: A Review (M. Paranthaman and B.C. Chakoumakos - Oak Ridge National Laboratory, Oak Ridge, TN.); Chapter 6: Mercury Cuprate High-Tc Superconductors: What Do Their Magnetic Properties Reveal? (James R Thompson - Oak Ridge National Laboratory, Oak Ridge, TN. and University of Tennessee, Knoxville); Chapter 7: Synthesis and Characterization of Bulk Hg $Ba_2Ca_{n-1}Cu_nO_{2n+2+\delta}$ (n= 1,2,3,4) Superconductors (M. Paranthaman and B.C. Chakoumakos); Chapter 8: Preparation of Superconducting Hg-Based Cuprate Thin Films By Means of Annealing of Mercury-Free Precursor Films (J.D. Guo, Y.F. Sun, X.L. Xu, G.C. Xiong, Z.H. Hu, C.W. Gao and W.H. Zhao - Dept of Physics, Peking University, Beijing); Chapter 9: Electronic Structure and the Van Hove Singularity Scenario in High Tc $HgBa_2Ca_{n-1}Cu_{2n+2+\delta}$ Superconductors: Pressure Effects (Bal K. Agrawal - Allahabad University, Iindia); Index

[C]Rapp, Östen.
Experimental studies of superconductivity in alloy systems.
[Stockholm, 1970?]
QC612.S8R3

[C]Raveau, B.
Crystal chemistry of high Tc superconducting copper oxides / B. Raveau ... [et al.].
Berlin ; New York : Springer-Verlag, c1991.
QC611.98.H54C79 1991

[C]Ribault, Michel; Moradpour, Alex; Organic superconducting thin films generated at a single crystal-solution interface; Journal of the American Chemical Society.v. 120 no31 Aug. 12 '98 p. 7993-4.
Electrocrystallization of TMTSF2ClO4 (TMTSF = tetramethyltetraselenafulvalene) at 40[degree]C resulted in the formation of a significant quantity of single crystals on the cell walls at sites remote from the Pt electrode. Superconducting TMTSF2ClO4 deposits were also grown by introducing, as a seed, a single crystal of the isostructural low-temperature narrow-gap semiconductor TMTSF2PF6 into a solution containing TMTSF and n-Bu4N+ClO4-.The resistance of single crystals prepared by these 2 methods as a function of temperature and as a function of the magnetic field was examined.

[C]Rice, Maurice; An analogue of superfluid 3He; Nature.v. 396 no6712 Dec. 17 '98 p. 627-9.
A complete description of the unconventional superconductivity of strontium ruthenate (Sr2RuO4) is now available. Articles by other authors in previous issues and a report by Ishida et al. in this issue have established that the superconductivity of Sr2RuO4 conforms to long-held views on how superconductivity driven by electron-electron interactions should behave.

[C]Roberts, Benjamin Washington, 1922-
Superconductive materials and some of their properties [by]B. W. Roberts. A report prepared for the Office of Standard Reference Data, Institute for Basic Standards, National Bureau of Standards, Washington, D.C.
[Washington]U.S. Dept. of Commerce, National Bureau of Standards; for sale by the Superintendent of Documents, U.S. Govt. Print. Off., 1966.
QC100.U5753 no. 408

[C]Roberts, Benjamin Washington, 1922-
Superconductive materials and some of their properties [by]B. W. Roberts.
Washington, U.S. Dept. of Commerce, National

Bureau of Standards; for sale by the Supt. of Docs., U.S.
Govt. Print. Off., 1969.
QC100.U5753 no. 482

[C]Salsgiver, J.A.,
Hard and soft magnetic materials with applications including superconductivity : proceedings of a conference on hard and soft magnetic materials held in conjunction with ASM's Materials Week '87, Cincinnati, Ohio, 10-15 October 1987
[Metals Park, Ohio] : ASM International, c1987.
TK454.4.M3H34 1987

[C]Savitskii, E. M.
Metallovedenie sverkhprovodëiiashchikh materialov. English
Superconducting materials [by]E. M. Savitskii [and others]. Translated from Russian by G. D. Archard. Translation editor K. D. Timmerhaus.
New York, Plenum Press [1973]
TN693.S9M413

[C]Scott, Bruce A; Kirtley, John R; Walker, David; Application of scanning SQUID petrology to high-pressure materials science; Nature.v. 389 Sept. 11 '97 p. 164-7.
A methodology combining the use of a scanning SQUID microscope with petrological techniques was used to image and identify low concentrations of superconducting phases in complex phase assemblages. To investigate the origin of superconductivity in the high-pressure Sr-Cu-O system, an Sr_2CuO_3 + $KClO_3$ diffusion couple was used to produce the superconductor $Sr_3Cu_2O_5Cl$. Scanning SQUID petrography demonstrated that this superconductor owes its existence to the unexpected involvement of Cl_2 from the ostensibly inert oxidizer.

[C]Seo, Dong Kyun; Ren, Jingqing; Whangbo, Myung Hwan; Electronic band structure study of the transport properties of the intermetallic compounds ZrRuP and ZrRuSi; Inorganic Chemistry.v. 36 Dec. 17 '97 p. 6058-63.
Electrical properties of the intermetallic superconductors h-ZrRuP, o-ZrRuP, and h-ZrRuSi were examined by calculating their electronic structures on the basis of the extended Huckel tight-binding method. This picture provides simple explanations for why both h-ZrRuP and o-ZrRuP have low N(Ef) values and why h-ZrRuP has a nearly half-filled one-dimensional (1D) band dispersive along the c direction. A charge density wave instability associated with such a 1D band probably causes a c-axis doubling structural distortion in h-HfRuAs and h-TiRuAs. The authors discussed probable reasons for why the intermetallic phases with the c-axis doubling distortion are not superconductors and why h-ZrRuP has a higher Tc than does o-ZrRuP. Copyright 1997,

[C]Service, Robert F.; Materials researchers pick up the pace of discovery; Science.v. 278 Dec. 19 '97 p. 2056-7.
Speed was a common theme among some 4,400 scientists who assembled in Boston between December 1 and 5, 1997, for the fall meeting of the Materials Research Society. Highlights of the meeting included a rapid-fire approach for developing and testing hundreds of slightly different electronic devices at the same time, a quicker method of making high-temperature superconducting wires, and a fast approach to durable coatings. Each of these is discussed.

[C]Service, Robert F; Insulator's baby steps to superconductivity; Science.v. 282 no5396 Dec. 11 '98 p. 1966-7.
In this issue, researchers suggest that the parent materials of superconductors are not as conservative as believed. Layered ceramic insulators cannot conduct electricity, but their superconductor offspring conduct electricity without any resistance.

[C]Shindé, Subhash L. , David A. Rudman
Interfaces in high-Tc superconducting systems /
Subhash L. Shindé, David A. Rudman, editors.
New York : Springer-Verlag, c1994.
QC611.98.H54I56 1994

[C]Simon Foner and Brian B. Schwartz.
NATO Advanced Study Institute on the Science and Technology of Superconducting Materials (1980 : Sintra, Portugal)
Superconductor materials science : metallurgy, fabrication, and applications / edited by Simon Foner and Brian B. Schwartz.
New York : Plenum Press, c1981.
TK454.4.S93N27 1980

[C]Sittig, Marshall.
Superconducting materials 1970 [by]Paul Conrad.
Park Ridge, N.J., Noyes Data Corp. [1970]
TK7872.S8S58

[C]Sólyom, J. (Jenö)
Theory of electron-electron interaction and superconductivity in dilute magnetic alloys above the Kondo temperature
[by] J. Sólyom and A. Zawadowski.
Budapest, Hungarian Academy of Sciences, Central Research Institute for Physics [1969]
QC1.M23 1969, no. 6

[C]Soulen, R. J., Jr; Byers, J. M; Osofsky, M. S.; Measuring the spin polarization of a metal with a superconducting point contact; Science.v. 282 no5386 Oct. 2 '98 p. 85-8. A superconducting point contact is used to determine the spin polarization at the Fermi energy of several metals. Because the process of supercurrent conversion at a superconductor-metal interface (Andreev reflection) is limited by the minority spin population near the Fermi surface, the differential conductance of the point contact can reveal the spin polarization of the metal.

[C]Spiewak, Mildred, 1930-
Magnetic field dependence of the surface
impedance of superconducting tin [microform]/ by Mildred
Spiewak. 1959.
Microfilm 6774 (Q)

[C]Studies of High Temperature Superconductors Volume 16.
Synthesis, High Pressure Effects and Some Miscellaneous Aspects
Anant Narlikar (Ed.)
1995. 307 pp. ISBN 1-56072-251-7. $110
Contents: Chapter 1: Recent Progress in High Pressure Investigation for High Tc Superconductors. H. Takahashi and N. Mori. Chapter 2: High Pressure Synthesis of Superconducting Cuprates with 1212- and 1222- Type Structures. Akira Ono and Shigeo Horiuchi, Chapter 3: Physico-Chemical Investigation of Crystal Growth of Superconducting YBa 2 Cu 3 0 7-y Chen Changkang, Chapter 4: Phase Evolution During the Fabrication of Bulk Bi-Based Superconducting Glass Ceramics. S. Mollah, N. Froumin and J. Baram, . Chapter 5: Superconductivity and Stoichiometry in the Electron-Doped L 2-x M x CuO 4 Oxides. J. Fontcuberta and L. Fabrega, Chapter 6: Optical Properties of Bi 2 Sr 2 Ca n-1CunO 4+2n+• • and the Related Compounds I. Terasaki, K. Uchinokura, Chapter 7: Phenomenon of Photoinduced Superconductivity: From Theoretical Prediction to Experimental Discoveries

[C]Studies of High Temperature Superconductors. Volume 10
Anant Narlikar (Ed.)
1992. 345 pages. ISBN 1-56072-087-5. $145.
Superconductivity; Physics; Chemistry; Materials Science; Solid State Engineering
Contents: Studies of Bi-Based High Tc Cuprates using High Resolution STM/STS Techniques; Far-Infrared Spectroscopy of High Temperature Superconductors; Magnetically Modulated Resistance Methods: Applications to Superconductors; A Review of Preparation Techniques for Bulk High Tc Superconductors; Flux Penetration and Critical Currents in High Tc Ceramics; Dependence of the Superconductivity of the Layered Cuprates on the Cu-O Charge-Transfer Energy and Related Chemical Bonding Parameters; Crystal Structure and Magnetic Properties in La4Ba2Cu2O10; Preparation of Y-Ba-Cu-O Superconductors by Freeze-Drying Method; Fabrication of Multilayered Thin Films with Bi-Based Superconductors and Their Superconducting Properties; Origin of Spin Susceptibility in High Temperature Superconductors: ESR and Static

Susceptibilitie; Electron Microscopy Investigations of Irradiation Defect Structures in High Tc Superconductor YBa2Cu3O7-x.

[C]Studies of High Temperature Superconductors. Volume 11
Anant Narlikar (Ed.)
1993. 467 pages. ISBN 1-56072-132-4. $135.
Superconductivity, Solid State
This is the eleventh volume of the internationally-acclaimed "Studies" in which there are 13 chapters covering some of the frontal areas of scientific and technical research of high temperature superconductors.Contents: Chapter-1: Scanning Tunelling Microscopy Of High Temperature Superconductors; Chapter-2: The Electronic Structure Of The New High Tc Superconductors Investigated By Core Level Absorption Spectroscopies Chapter-3: Magnetization And Critical State Models For Hard Superconductors; Chapter-4: Neutron Studies Of Excess Oxygen In High Tc Bi-Cuprates And Substituted Phases; Chapter-5: Superconductivity In Strongly Disordered Systems; Chapter-6: Optical Properties In Marginal Fermi Liquid Theory; Chapter-7: Theory Of Electronic Structure Of High-Tc Superconductors: Doping Dependence Of Density Of States And Magnetism; Chapter-8: Static And Dynamic Properties Of Vortex States In Type-Ii Superconductors; Chapter-9: Tight Binding Method For Correlated Electrons With Particular Attention To High-T Superconductors; Chapter-10: Synthesis And Characterization Of Tl2Ba2CuO6 Systems - A Review; Chapter-11 Resistive States And Some Peculiarities Of Their Evolution In Hts-Composites With Current Chapter-12: Structural And Microstructural Characteristics Of High Temperature Superconducting Cuprates In Relation To Tc And Jc Optimization Chapter-13: High Resolution Transmission Electron Microscope Studies Of Planar Defects In YBa2Cu4Oy Superconductors Doped With Ca, Co, Fe

[C]Studies of High Temperature Superconductors. Volume 2
A.V. Narlikar (Ed.)
1989. 370 pages, $145. ISBN 0-941743-55-1.
Superconductivity, Physics, Chemistry, Materials Science, Solid State Electronics, Engineeering
Contents: Structural Chemistry Of High Tc Superconductors; High Pressure Studies; Nuclear Resonance Studies $Inyba_2cu_3o_x$ And $Tl_2ba_2ca_2$-Cu_3o_{10+X}; Thermal Properties Of High Temperature Superconductors); Phonons In High Tc Superconductors; A Review Of The Preparation And Structure Of Bi-Sr-Ca-Cu-O Superconductors And Pb-Substituted Phases; Anisotropic Superconducting And Normal State Transport Properties Of Htsc Single Crystals; Multiple Heteroepitaxial Growth Of High Tc Superconductors; Coprecipitation Route To Ceramic Superconductors; Microwave Absorption Studies In High Tc Superconducting Oxides; X-Ray Spectroscopic Study Of High Temperature Superconductors; Normal And Superconducting Properties Of The New High Tc Oxides And The Phonon-Plasmon Mechanism Of Superconductivity; Magnetic Pairing And Superconductivity; Low Dimensionality Aspects Of High Temperature Superconductors; Theory Of High Temperature Superconductivity.

[C]Studies of High Temperature Superconductors. Volume 3
A.V. Narlikar (Ed.)
1989. 413 pages, $145. ISBN 0-941743-56-X.
Superconductivity, Physics, Chemistry, Materials Science, Solid State Electronics, Engineeering
Contents: Charge-Fluctuation Excitations as Mechanisms for High Tc; High Resolution Electron Microscopy Study of High Tc Superconductors; Synthesis of High Temperature Superconducting Films-Processing Science and Issues; Effect of Oxygen Ordering on the Superconductivity of $Y_1Ba_2Cu_3O_{7-\_}$; On the Architecture of High Tc Superconductors; Thermally Activated Magnetic Relaxation in High Tc Superconductors; Magnetizationof Single Crystalline and Grain Aligned High Tc Superconductors; Synthesis of Bulk Sintered Samples, Processing and Crystal Growth of $YBa_2Cu_3O_7$; Superconducting Weak Links in High Tc Superconductors; Ginzburg-Landau Theory for High-Tc Superconductors; BCS Like Approach to HTSC With Emphasis on Structural Transformation; Vibrational Spectra and Transport Properties of High Temperature Superconductors; Twins in High Tc Superconductors; Structure, Microstructure and Superconductivity in the Thallium-Based Oxide Superconductors; Micro-structural Characteristics and Structure-Property Correlations in High Temperature Superconductors.

[C]Studies of High Temperature Superconductors. Volume 4
A.V. Narlikar (Ed.)
1989. 402 pages, $145. ISBN 0-941743-57-8.
Superconductivity, Physics, Chemistry, Materials Science, Solid State Electronics, Engineeering
Contents: Weak Coupling Theory of High Temperature Superconductor; Investigations of a few Novel Series of Thallium Cuprate Superconductors Showing Possible Change in the Sign of Charge Carriers with Composition; Some Structural and Chemical Aspects of the Bi-Pb-Sr-Ca-Cu-O System; High Magnetic Field Studies of High Temperature Superconductors; Fabrication of Bi-Sr-Ca-Cu Oxide Superconductors with Controlled Numbers of Cu-O Layers; Characterization of High Temperature Superconductors by High Excitation Spectroscopies; Mössbauer Spectroscopy of High Temperature Superconductors; RVB and Related Theories of HTSC; Fabrication of 107K Superconducting Films and their Normal State Transport Properties; Ion Beam Analysis of High Tc Superconductors; Thermal Conductivity of High Temperature Superconductors; A New Theoretical Approach to Electron Pairing and Superconductivity in High Tc Superconductors; High Resolution Polarized X-ray Absorption Spectroscopy: Symmetry of the Hole States in High-Tc Superconductors; Phase Diagrams in the Y-Ba-Cu-O System and Crystal Growth of YBCO Superconductors.

[C]Studies of High Temperature Superconductors. Volume 5
A.V. Narlikar (Ed.)
1990. 413 pages, $150. ISBN 0-941743-87-X.
Superconductivity, Physics, Chemistry, Materials Science, Solid State Electronics, Engineeering
Contents: •Quest for the High Tc Mechanism in Copper-Oxide Superconductors; •Neutron Scattering Studies of Magnetism in High Tc Materials; •Flux Pinning and Thermally Activated Depinning in Single Crystals of High Temperature Superconductors; •Some Model Mechanisms for High Temperature Superconductors;•Chemistry and Superconductivity of Thallium-Based Cuprates; •Preparation and Properties of Superconducting Ceramics and Films in the System Bi-(Pb)-Sr-Ca-Cu-O (G.; •Relaxation Properties and Critical Currents in Bi-Sr-Ca-Cu-O Single Crystals; •Formation Processes of Polycrystalline Superconducting Copper Oxides; •High Resolution Transmission Electron Microscope Study of Modulated Structures in Bismuth-Based Superconductors; •Studies of Superconducting Energy Gap in High Temperature Superconductors; •Recent Techniques of Fabricating High Tc Superconductors; •Critical Current Problem in High Tc Superconductors; •Microstructure Property Relationships in the Bi(Pb).

[C]Studies of High Temperature Superconductors. Volume 7
A.V. Narlikar (Ed.)
398 pages, 1991. $145. ISBN 1-56072-007-7.
Superconductivity; Physics Chemistry; Material Science; Solid State Engineering
Contents: Preparation and Properties of High-Jc Bi-Sr-Ca-Cu-O Tape Conductors; Oxide Melt Fast Solidification as a Route to Prepare HTS; Studies of Electron-Beam Deposited Thin Films of the Thallium-Based High Tc Cuprates; Film-Substrate Interactions in High Tc Superconducting Thin Films; Electronic and Magnetic Structure of High Tc Cuprates and Nickelates; Correlated Electrons, Flux States and Superconductivity; A Unified Statistical Mechanical Approach to High Temperature Superconductivity; Magnetic, Transport and Microwave Properties of $YBa_2Cu_3O_7$ Thin Films; Oxygen Behaviour in 1-2-3 Compounds; Fluorination of High Tc Superconductors; Thermoelectricity of High Temperature Superconductors.

[C]Suhl, Harry, M. Brian Maple
Conference on Superconductivity in d-and f-Band Metals (1979 : University of California, San Diego)
Superconductivity in d- and f-band metals /
New York : Academic Press, 1980.
QC610.9.C63 1979

[C]Sung H. Whang, Amit DasGupta
Symposium on High Temperature Superconducting
Oxides: Processing & Related Properties (1989 : Las Vegas, Nev.)
High temperature superconducting compounds :

processing & related properties : proceedings of the 1989 Symposium on High Temperature Superconducting Oxides--Processing & Related Properties, which was sponsored by the Superconducting Materials Committee and held in Las Vegas, NV, February 27 and 28, 1989, at the 118th Annual Meeting of the Minerals, Metals & Materials Society / edited by Sung H. Whang, Amit DasGupta.
Warrendale, Pa. : The Society, c1989.
QC611.98.H54S95 1989

[C]Sung H. Whang, Amit DasGupta, and Edward Collings
High temperature superconducting compounds III : processing and microstructure property relationships : proceedings of a symposium by the Superconducting Materials Committee, the Structural Materials Division and the Electronic Materials Division of the Minerals, Metals, and Materials Society, New Orleans, Louisiana, February, 1991 / edited by Sung H. Whang, Amit DasGupta, and Edward Collings.
Warrendale, Pa. : Minerals, Metals & Materials Society, c1991.
QC611.98.H54H5423 1991

[C]Sung H. Whang, Amit DasGupta, Robert Laibowitz
High temperature superconducting compounds II / edited by Sung H. Whang, Amit DasGupta, Robert Laibowitz.
Warrendale, Pa. : Minerals, Metals & Materials Society, c1990.
QC611.98.H54H542 1990

[C]Superconductivity and related new materials : report / by the House of Representatives Standing Committee on Industry, Science and Technology.
Canberra : Australian Govt. Pub. Service, c1988.
J905.L3 1988, no. 326; Alternative class.:
QC611.96

[C]Thermal Properties and Some Miscellaneous Aspects of High Temperature Superconductors.
(Volume 19 of Studies of High Temperature Superconductors)
Anant Narlikar (Ed.).
1996. 262 pages. ISBN 1-56072-393-9. $110.
Contents: Specific Heat Of High Temperature Superconductors In High Magnetic Fields; (A. Junod, Universite De Geneve); Elastic Behavior Of Some High Tc Superconductors; (P. Venugopal Reddy,Osmania University); Specific Heat And Other Related Studies On Pure And Substituted Phases Of Hightc Cuprates; (A.K. Bandyopadhyay, National Physical Laboratory); Thermal Analysis Of High Tc Superconductors; (Tamalika

Bandyopadhyay, V. Sridharan, D. Ravichandran, S, Sivasankaran, D.K. Biswas And T. Nagarajan, Department Of Nuclear Physics, University Of Madras); The Anomalous Metallic Phase And High Tc Superconductivity Of Copper Oxides; M. Sato (Department Of Physics, Division Of Materials Science, Nagoya University); Investigation Of Effect And Mechanisms Of Low-Energy Neutron Irradiation Of High Tc Superconductors; (Ji-Rong Jin And Xin Jin, Department Of Physics, State Key Laboratory Of Solid State Microstructures, Nanjing 210008, China).

[C]Vanderah, Terrell A.
Chemistry of superconductor materials :
preparation, chemistry, characterization, and theory / edited
by Terrell A. Vanderah.
Park Ridge, N.J. : Noyes Publications, c1992.
QC611.97.C54C48 1991

[C]Vonsovskiæi, S. V. (Sergeæi Vasil§evich)
Sverkhprovodimost§ perekhodnykh metallov, ikh
splavov i soedineniæi. English
Superconductivity of transition metals : their
alloys and compounds / S.V. Vonsovsky, Yu. A. Izyumov, E.Z.
Kurmaev ; translation by E.H. Brandt and A.P. Zavarnitsyn.
Berlin ; New York : Springer-Verlag, 1982.
QC612.S8V6613 1982

[C]Waldram, J. R.
Superconductivity of metals and cuprates / J.R. Waldram.
Bristol ; Philadelphia, Pa. : Institute of
Physics Pub., c1996.
QC611.92.W35 1996

[C]Waldram, J. R; Cohen, L. F., reviewer; Superconductivity of metals and cuprates (book review); Contemporary Physics.v. 40 no1 Jan./Feb. '99 p. 90-1. .
[C]Waldram, J. R; Goldman, Allen M., reviewer; Superconductivity of metals and cuprates (book review); Physics Today.v. 50 Aug. '97 pt 1 p. 58+. .

[C]Walter, John L.
Structure & property relationships for interfaces
/ edited by John L. Walter, Alexander H. King, Kris Tangri.
[Materials Park, Ohio]: ASM International, c1991.
TA455.C43S775 1991

[C]William E. Hatfield, John H. Miller, Jr
High-temperature superconducting materials :
preparations, properties, and processing / edited by William
E. Hatfield, John H. Miller, Jr.

New York : M. Dekker, c1988.
TK7872.S8H54 1988

[C]Yamanaka, Shoji; Hotehama, Ken ichi; Kawaji, Hitoshi; Superconductivity at 25.5 K in electron-doped layered hafnium nitride; Nature.v. 392 no6676 Apr. 9 '98 p. 580-2.
The isostructural compound b-HfNCl was characterized. Superconductivity with a transition temperature of up to 25.5 K was observed when the crystal was electron doped with lithium intercalation. This transition temperature is higher than that seen in any intermetallic compound. Thus, layered nitride structures may offer transition temperatures comparable with those exhibited by layered copper oxide structures.

[C]Yoshizawa, Kazunari; Kato, Takashi; Tachibana, Masamitsu; Vibronic interactions in silicon polyhedra of the Si46 clathrate compound; The Journal of Physical Chemistry A.v. 102 no49 Dec. 3 '98 p. 10113-19.
The vibronic (vibrational-electronic) interactions in the Si46 clathrate compound are discussed using the highly symmetric (SiH)20 and (SiH)24 cluster models to look at a possible correlation between the Jahn-Teller effect and the superconductivity. The vibronic coupling constants for six Hg modes in the mono-, tri-, and pentaanions of (SiH)20 and for twelve E4 modes in the tri- and pentaanions of (SiH)24 are calculated using the MNDO-PM3 method, one of the most reliable semiempirical molecular orbital methods, to know which mode of vibration plays a governing role in the Jahn-Teller distortions of these hypothetical multianions.

Applications

[D]A Proposal to site the superconducting super
collider in Lenawee and Monroe counties, Michigan / submitted
to United States Department of Energy by the State of
Michigan, Superconducting Super Collider Commission.
[Lansing]: The Commission, [1987]
QC787.P7P76 1987

[D]A Superconducting magnet for fusion research.
[Motion picture]
QC757

[D]Abe, Fumio, Katsuo Hasegawa
International Workshop on Solenoidal Detectors
for the SSC (1990 : Tsukuba-shi, Japan)
Proceedings of the International Workshop on
Solenoidal Detectors for the SSC, April 23-25, 1990, KEK,
Tsukuba, Japan / edited by Fumio Abe, Katsuo Hasegawa.
Tsukuba-shi, Japan : KEK, National Laboratory for
High Energy Physics, c1990.
QC787.P7I58 1990

[D]Akopëiian, D. G. (Dorvard Gurgenovich)
Upravlenie i zashchita sverkhprovodnikovykh
magnitnykh sistem / D.G. Akopëiian, D.M. Lerner.
Leningrad : çEnergoatomizdat, Leningradskoe otd-nie, 1991.
TK7872.S8A43 1991

[D]Al'tov, V. A.
Stabilizaëtìsiëiia sverkhprovodëiiashchikh
magnitnykh sistem
Stabilization of superconducting magnetic systems
/ V. A. Al'tov ... [et al.]; edited by V. V. Sychev ;
translated from Russian by G. D. Archard ; translation
editor, K. D. Timmerhaus ; with a foreword by B. W. Birmingham.
New York : Plenum Press, c1977.
QC761.3.S713

[D]Applied superconductivity.
Oxford ; New York : Pergamon, c1992-
TK7872.S8A667

[D]Barker, Brendan.
Superconductivity : a realistic appraisal of
technology, markets, and commercial potential / Brendan Barker.
Oxford, UK : Elsevier Advanced Technology, c1989.
TK454.4.S93B37 1989

[D]Barone, Antonio, Aususto Morini, Luigi Frunzio
School on European Training on Technologies and
Industrial Applications of Superconductivity (1st : 1991 : Naples, Italy)
Ettias, 1st School on European Training on
Technologies and Industrial Applications of
Superconductivity, Naples, Italy, 9-13 September 1991 /
Singapore ; River Edge, N.J. : World Scientific, c1992.
TK7872.S8S33 1991

[D]Battersby, Stephen; Cold cousin of the colloids; Nature.v. 392 no6678 Apr. 16 '98 p. 660.
Recent advances in the study of superconductor vortices are described. Some conductors admit magnetic fields in thin flux lines, or vortices, which can cause electrical resistance. High-resolution videos of vortex motion were made by a Japanese group led by Akira Tonomura in the hope of understanding how defects in superconductors manage to pin vortices down. Sow et al. (Phys. Rev. Lett. 1998;80:2693-6) adapted new data-analysis techniques for application to these videos in order to measure the strength of vortex-vortex interactions and the distribution of pinning potentials.

[D]Baus, Wolfgang W.
Magnetic anomaly detection using conventional and
superconductive sensors with respect to vehicle monitoring /
Wolfgang W. Baus.
Bochum : Brockmeyer, 1995.
UG615.B38 1995

[D]Bengtsson, H.-U.
Observable standard model physics at the SSC :
Monte Carlo simulation and detector capabilities :
proceedings of the UCLA workshop, 15-24 January 1986 / edited
by H.-U. Bengtsson ... [et al].
Singapore ; [Philadelphia]: World Scientific, c1986.
QC787.P7O27 1986

[D]Bozovic, Ivan, Davor Pavuna
Oxide superconductor physics and nano-engineering
II : 30 January -2 February, San Jose, California / Ivan
Bozovic, Davor Pavuna, chairs/editors ; sponsored by
SPIE--the International Society for Optical Engineering ...

[et al.]; published by SPIE--The International Society for Optical Engineering.
Bellingham, Wash., USA : SPIE, c1996.
QC611.98.H54O95 1996

[D]Bozovic, Ivan, Davor Pavuna
Superconducting superlattices II, native and artificial : 20-22 July 1998, San Diego, California / Ivan Bozovic, Davor Pavuna, chairs/editors ; sponsored and published by SPIE--the International Society for Optical Engineering ; cosponsored by Oxxel GmbH Bremen (Germany).
Bellingham, Wash. : SPIE, c1998.
QC611.94.S88 1998

[D]Brechna, H.
Superconducting magnet systems, by H. Brechna.
Berlin, New York, Springer, 1973.
QC760.7.B73

[D]Brown, Henry S. (Henry Seawell), 1930-
Superconducting Super Collider : appendix : petrography and photomicrographics / by Henry S. Brown.
[Raleigh, NC]: N.C. Geological Survey, Division of Land Resources, Department of Environment, Health and Natural Resources, 1997.
QC787.P7B76 1997

[D]Browne, Malcolm W.; Power line makes use of a miracle of physics; New York Times (Late New York Edition).Nov. 3 '98 p. F1-F2.
The world's first superconducting power line is about to become a reality. Superconducting lines are 2-5 times more efficient than ordinary copper wires, thus conserving energy. Indeed, energy secretary Bill Richardson predicted 2 weeks ago that superconducting power lines could eventually save the nation $6 billion a year. The new power line, which will be built by a consortium, is intended to serve an urban redevelopment project in Detroit, Michigan. Estimated to cost $5.5 million, the 400-feet-long line will be manufactured from a finely powdered mixture of bismuth, strontium, calcium, copper oxide, and lead. Operation should begin by mid-2000.

[D]Bumby, J. R. (James Richard)
Superconducting rotating electrical machines / J.R. Bumby.
Oxford [Oxfordshire]; New York : Clarendon Press, 1983.
TK2189.B85 1983

[D]Cabrera, Blas, H. Gutfreund, and Vladimir Kresin.
From high-temperature superconductivity to microminiature refrigeration

New York : Plenum Press, c1996.
QC611.98.H54F76 1996

[D]California. Legislature. Joint Committee on
Science and Technology.
Governor's proposals on collaborative research &
superconductivity : hearing, State of California, State
Capitol, Room 2040, Sacramento, California, Wednesday, June
15, 1988 / Joint Committee on Science and Technology and
Assembly Committee on Economic Development and New
Technologies ; reported by Evelyn Mizak.
Sacramento, CA : Joint Committee on Science and
Technology : Additional copies may be purchased from Joint
Publications, [1988]
KFC10.S35 1988c

[D]Cambridge Conference on Commercial Applications
of Superconductivity.
Proceedings / the ... Annual Cambridge Conference
on Commercial Applications of Superconductivity.
Cambridge, MA : World Tech Press, 1988-

[D]Chandra, J. and A.C. Scott
Coupled nonlinear oscillators : proceedings of
the Joint U.S. Army-Center for Nonlinear Studies workshop,
held in Los Alamos, New Mexico, 21-23 July, 1981 / edited by
J. Chandra and A.C. Scott.
Amsterdam ; New York : North-Holland ; New York :
Sole distributors for the U.S.A. and Canada, Elsevier Science, 1983.
TK7872.O7C65 1983

[D]Cheng-Chung (John) Chi, R. Bruce van Dover (eds.)
High Tc superconductivity, thin films and
applications : 20-21 March 1990, San Diego, California /
sponsored by SPIE--the International Society for Optical
Engineering, in cooperation with the Society of Vacuum Coaters.
Bellingham, Wash., USA : SPIE, c1990.
TK7872.T55H52 1990

[D]Chernoplekova, N.A.
Sverkhprovodëiìashchie magnitnye sistemy dlëiìa
tokamakov / pod redakëtìsieæi N.A. Chernoplekova.
Moskva : IzdAT, 1997.
TK9204.S85 1997

[D]Christen, David; Current limits to wire technology; Nature.v. 392 no6679 Apr. 30 '98 p. 862-3.
The authors describe experiments on single filaments extracted from a BiSrCaCuO superconductor (BSCCO) tape that shed light on the barriers to current flow in high-temperature superconductors. The BSCCO tapes are formed by loading a powder of BSCCO into a silver or silver-alloy tube that is then sealed and drawn into a fine wire. The wires are cut and restacked and are then subjected to a series of additional drawing, rolling, and heat-treatment steps, resulting in the final multifilament oxide-powder-in-tube tapes. Cai et al. demonstrate that a lot of the fine BSCCO filaments are not active because of the intrusion of cracks from the tape edges. They also produce evidence of some c-axis conduction, indicating that there are local barriers preventing basal-plane conduction.

[D]Cieâsla, Antoni.
Analiza stanów pracy separatora matrycowego z elektromagnesem nadprzewodnikowym jako âzródlem pola / Antoni Cieâsla.
Kraków : Wydawnictwa AGH, 1996.

[D]Claeys, Cor L.(ed.)
Symposium on Low Temperature Electronics and High Temperature Superconductivity (3rd : 1995 : Reno, Nevada)
Proceedings of the Symposium on Low Temperature Electronics and High Temperature Superconductivity / editors,
Pennington, NJ : Electrochemical Society, c1995.
QC611.98.H54S96 1995

[D]Cohen, Morrel H. (ed.)
Superconductivity in science and technology.
Chicago, University of Chicago Press [1968]
QC611.S937

[D]Collings, E. W.
Applied superconductivity, metallurgy, and physics of titanium alloys / E.W. Collings.
New York : Plenum Press, c1986.
TN693.T5C625 1986

[D]Commercializing high-temperature superconductivity.
Washington, DC : Congress of the U.S., Office of Technology Assessment : For sale by the Supt. of Docs., U.S. G.P.O., [1988]
TK7872.S8C65 1988

[D]Connaughton, John E.
The expected economic impacts and net revenue
benefits of locating the Superconducting Super Collider in
North Carolina / prepared by John E. Connaughton, Ronald A. Madsen.
[Charlotte, N.C.]: Center for Business and
Economic Research, University of North Carolina at Charlotte, [1988]
QC787.P7C66 1988

[D]Cooper, Leon N.
The physics and application of superconductivity
[by] Leon N. Cooper and Brian B. Schwartz.
New York, Technology Forecasting Institute, 1968.
QC612.S8C6

[D]Crabtree, George W; Nelson, David R.; Vortex physics in high-temperature superconductors; Physics Today.v. 50 Apr. '97 p. 38-45.
The discovery of high-temperature superconductors has encouraged dramatic growth in the understanding of the physics of quantized vortex lines, creating new horizons in fundamental science and potential commercial applications. Vortices in superconductors offer a highly accessible example of flexible one-dimensional objects interacting through a simple potential in the presence of controlled disorder. In addition, technology has embraced the potential of high-temperature superconductors, with over 15 companies actively involved in developing products ranging from high-current bulk wires and tapes to thin film devices.

[D]Critical Current , Flux Pinning and Optical Studies of High Temperature Superconductors
(Volume 22 in Studies of High Temperature Superconductors)
Anant Narlikar (Ed.)
1997, 278 pages, ISBN 1-56072-420-X. $110.
FLUX PINNING IN MELT-PROCESSED RE123 SUPERCONDUCTORS. M. Murakami. (International Superconductivity Technology Centre, Superconductivity Research Laboratory, Shibaura, Minato-ku, 105 Tokyo, JAPAN); CRITICAL CURRENT AND FLUX PINNING IN YBA2 CU3 OX CRYSTAL PREPARED BY MELT-TEXTURED GROWTH METHOD. C.D. Wei (a), H.T. Ren (b) and L. Xiao (b). (a) Department of Physics, Peking Univ., Beijing 100871, PEOPLES REPUBLIC OF CHINA). (b) General Research Inst.for Non-Ferrous Metal, Beijing, PEOPLES REPUBLIC OF CHINA); AC SUSCEPTIBILITY AND INTERGRANULAR CRITICAL STATE IN HIGH Tc SUPERCONDUCTORS . Du-Xiang Chen (a) and Alvaro Sanchez (b) (a) Instituto de Magnetismo Aplicado, RENFE-UCM, 28230 Las Rozas (Madrid), SPAIN.(b) Grup d'Electromagnetisme, Departamento de Fisica,. Universitat Autonoma Barcelona, 08193 Bellaterra (Barcelona), SPAIN. ELECTRONIC STATES OF HIGH Tc SUPERCONDUCTORS PROBED BY RADIATION INDUCED DISORDER. A. Karkin, V. Verkhovskii, V. Voronin, B. Goshchitskii and A.

Mirmelstein. (Inst.for Metal Physics, Russian Academy of Sciences, 620219 Ekaterinburg GSP-170, RUSSIA.). INFLUENCE OF LIGHT ON COPPER OXIDE SUPERCONDUCTORS. Reino Laiho (Wihuri Physical Laboratory, Univ. of Turku, 20500 Turku, FINLAND.) LOW TEMPERATURE OPTICAL SPECTROSCOPY OF YBaCuO THIN FILMS: CHARGE DYNAMICS IN NORMAL AND SUPERCONDUCTING STATES. (I.Ya. Fugol and V.N. Samovarov , B. Verkin Inst.for Low Temperature Physics and Engineering, National Academy Sciences of Ukraine, Kharkov, 310164 UKRAINE.)
THEORY OF ELECTRONIC RAMAN SCATTERING IN TWO DIMENSIONAL d-WAVE SUPERCONDUCTORS (D.J.Branch and J.P. Carbotte, Department of Physics and Astronomy, McMaster Univ., Hamilton, Ont., CANADA L8S 4M1.); LIGHT SCATTERING IN HIGH Tc (Y/Pr)Ba2Cu3O7 SUPERLATTICES (R. Li (a), E. Sherman (b) and R. Feile (c). (a) Department of Physics and Centre for Electro-Optics, Univ. of Nebraska-Lincoln, NE 68588-6111, U.S.A. (b) Moscow Inst.of Physics and Technology, 141700 Dolgoprudny, RUSSIA. (c) Institut fur Festkorperphysik Technische Hochschule Darmstadt, D-64289 Darmstadt, GERMANY. Subject Index

[D]Cyrot, M.
Introduction to superconductivity and high-Tc materials / Michel Cyrot, Davor Pavuna.
Singapore ; River Edge, N.J. : World Scientific, c1992.
QC611.92.C97 1992

[D]Daugherty, Debra; Superconductors in a twist; New Scientist.v. 157 no2120 Feb. 7 '98 p. 32-5.
Scientists are now working to resolve the conflict between superconductivity and self-magnetism that has condemned high-temperature superconductors to underachievement. In these materials, magnetic fields spoil superconductivity by forming thousands of microscopic swirling currents that cause great problems when they move about. By learning to control their motion, however, researchers are beginning to develop a peaceful coexistence between superconductivity and magnetism, enabling superconducting technology to finally realize its potential.

[D]De Sanctis, E.
Workshop on Heavy-Quark Factory and Nuclear-Physics Facility with Superconducting Linacs (1987 : Courmayeur, Italy)
Workshop on Heavy-Quark Factory and Nuclear-Physics Facility with Superconducting Linacs / edited by E. De Sanctis ... [et al.], 14-18 December 1987.
Bologna : Italian Physical Society, c1988.
QC793.5.Q252W67 1987

[D]Deaver, B. S.
Conference on Future Trends in Superconductive Electronics, Charlottesville, Va., 1978.
Future trends in superconductive electronics (Charlottesville, 1978) / editors, B. S. Deaver, Jr. ... [et al.].
New York : American Institute of Physics, 1978.
TK7872.S8C66 1978

[D]Deutscher, Guy.
Superconductivity and cryogenics / by Guy Deutscher.
Jerusalem : Prime Minister's Office, National Council for Research and Development, 1976.
TK454.4.S93D48

[D]Di Giacomo, Joseph
VLSI handbook : silicon, gallium arsenide, and superconductor circuits / Joseph Di Giacomo, editor in chief.
New York : McGraw-Hill, c1989.
TK7874.V563 1989

[D]Dombeck, Tom, Valerie Kelly, and George P. Yost
Symposium on Detector Research and Development for the Superconducting Super Collider (1990 : Fort Worth, Tex.)
Proceedings of the Symposium on Detector Research and Development for the Surperconducting Super Collider, October 15-18, 1990, Fort Worth, Texas / editors, Tom Dombeck, Valerie Kelly, and George P. Yost; sponsored by Superconducting Super Collider Laboratory, United States Department of Energy, and Universities Research Association, Inc.
Singapore ; Teaneck, N.J. : World Scientific, 1991.
QC787.P7S96 1990

[D]Donaldson, Rene and Jay Marx
Summer Study on the Physics of the Superconducting Supercollider (1986 : Snowmass, Colo.)
Proceedings of the 1986 Summer Study on the Physics of the Superconducting Supercollider, June 23-July 11, 1986 / editors, Rene Donaldson and Jay Marx ; organized by the Division of Particles and Fields of the American Physical Society ; sponsored jointly by the Division of Particles and Fields of the American Physical Society ... [et al.].
[New York, N.Y.]: The Division, 1986.
QC787.P7S865 1986

[D]Donaldson, Rene and M.G.D. Gilchriese.
Workshop on Experiments, Detectors, and
Experimental Areas for the Supercollider (1987 : University
of California, Berkeley)
Proceedings of the Workshop on Experiments,
Detectors, and Experimental Areas for the Supercollider :
July 7-17, 1987, Berkeley, California / editors, Rene
Donaldson and M.G.D. Gilchriese.
Teaneck, N.J. : World Scientific, c1988.
QC787.P7W67 1987

[D]Eckels, P.W., K.M. Obasih
American Society of Mechanical Engineers. Winter
Meeting (1992 : Anaheim, Calif.)
Heat transfer in superconducting equipment :
presented at the Winter Annual Meeting of the American
Society of Mechanical Engineers, Anaheim, California,
November 8-13, 1992 / sponsored by the Heat Transfer
Division, ASME ; edited by P.W. Eckels, K.M. Obasih.
New York, N.Y. : American Society of Mechanical
Engineers, c1992.
TK7872.S8A45 1992

[D]Ehsani, Mehrdad.
Converter circuits for superconductive magnetic
energy storage / by Mehrdad Ehsani and Robert L. Kustom.
College Station : Published for the Texas
Engineering Experiment Station by Texas A&M University Press, c1988.
TK2985.E37 1988

[D]Ehsani, Mehrdad.
Converter circuits for superconductive magnetic
energy storage / by Mehrdad Ehsani and Robert L. Kustom.
College Station : Published for the Texas
Engineering Experiment Station by Texas A&M University Press, c1988.
TK2985.E37 1988

[D]Electric energy systems : current abstracts /
U.S. Department of Energy ; prepared for Office of
Conservation and Renewable Energy ; prepared by Office of
Scientific and Technical Information.
Oak Ridge, TN : The Office of Scientific and
Technical Information, [c1988-

[D]Electric energy systems. Superconductivity
applications : current abstracts / U.S. Department of Energy
prepared for Office of Energy Efficiency and Renewable

Energy, Office of Utility Technologies ; prepared by Office
of Scientific and Technical Information.
Oak Ridge, TN : U.S. Dept. of Energy, c1994-

[D]Forbes, Donn.
The U.S. market for high-temperature
superconducting wire in transmission cable applications /
conducted by Donn Forbes as part of the Superconductivity
Partnership Initiative under contract with the National
Renewable Energy Laboratory.
Golden, CO : National Renewable Energy
Laboratory, April 1996.
TK3251.F67 1996

[D]G. G. Schastlivyæi, A. I. Titko, G. M. Fedorenko, V. P. Kovalenko
Instytut elektrodynamiky (Akademiëìa nauk
Ukraïns'koï RSR)
Nadezhnost' sovremennykh i perspektivnykh
turbogeneratorov / Akademiëìa nauk Ukrainskoæi SSR, Institut
çelektrodinamiki ; [G. G. Schastlivyæi, A. I. Titko, G. M.
Fedorenko, V. P. Kovalenko]; Pod red. G. G. Schastlivogo.
Kiev : Nauk. dumka, 1978.
TK2765.A42 1978

[D]G. Waysand and G. Chardin
Symposium C on Superconducting and
Low-Temperature Particle Detectors (1988 : Strasbourg, France)
Superconducting and low-temperature particle
detectors : proceedings of Symposium C on Superconducting and
Low-Temperature Particle Detectors of the 1988 E-MRS Fall
Conference, Strasbourg, France, 8-10 November 1988 / edited
by G. Waysand and G. Chardin.
Amsterdam ; New York : North-Holland ; New York,
N.Y., USA : Distributors for the U.S.A. and Canada, Elsevier
Science Pub. Co., 1989.
QC785.5.S97 1988

[D]Gallop, J. C. (John C.)
SQUIDS, the Josephson effects and superconducting
electronics / J.C. Gallop.
Bristol, England ; Philadelphia : Adam Hilger, c1991.
TK7872.S8G35 1990

[D]Garwin, Laura; Superconductors make their public debut in US utility network;
Nature.v. 395 no6704 Oct. 22 '98 p. 733.
This week, the Department of Energy announced the first project to install high-

temperature superconducting (HTS) power cables in a utility network. In a $5.5-million demonstration project jointly funded by the department and private industry, underground copper cables in an electricity substation in Detroit, Michigan, will be replaced by three 130-meter-long HTS cables in 2 years' time. The participants in the project are optimistic that it will be a stepping stone to the large-scale commercialization of the high-temperature oxide superconductors discovered for the first time 12 years ago.

[D]Geological-geotechnical studies for siting the superconducting super collider in Illinois : preliminary geological feasibility report / J.P. Kempton ... [et al.].
Champaign, Ill. : Illinois State Geological Survey, 1985.
QE105.A32 no. 111; Alternative class.: QE106.B37

[D]Geological-geotechnical studies for siting the superconducting super collider in Illinois : results of the 1986 test drilling program / B.B. Curry ... [et al.].
Champaign, Ill. (615 E. Peabody Dr., Champaign 61820) : Dept. of Energy and Natural Resources, Illinois State Geological Survey, 1988.
QE105.A32 no. 122; Alternative class.: QE106.B37

[D]Geotechnical summary to the proposal to site the superconducting super collider in Illinois / prepared by Harza Engineering Company with assistance of ISGS.
[Champaign, IL]: Dept. of Energy and Natural Resources, Illinois State Geological Survey, 1988.
QE106.B37G46 1988

[D]Gidrodinamika i teploobmen v sverkhprovodnikovykh ustroæistvakh / otvetstvennye redaktory Z.L. Miropol'skii, R.I. Soziev.
Moskva : "Nauka", 1990.
TK7871.85G45 1990

[D]Giovannella, C. M. Tinkham
Macroscopic quantum phenomena and coherence in superconducting networks : Frascati, Italy, 2-5 March 1995 / editors, C. Giovannella, M. Tinkham.
Singapore ; New Jersey : World Scientific, c1995.
TK7872.S8M33 1995

[D]Giovannella, C. , M. Tinkham
Macroscopic quantum phenomena and coherence in superconducting networks : Frascati, Italy, 2-5 March 1995 / editors, C. Giovannella, M. Tinkham.
Singapore ; New Jersey : World Scientific, c1995.
TK7872.S8M33 1995

[D]Girard, T.A. , A. Morales, and G. Waysand (eds.).
Superconductivity and particle detection :
Toledo, Spain, April 20-24, 1994,
Singapore ; River Edge, NJ : World Scientific, c1995.
QC787.C6S8 1995

[D]Glazer, Herbert.
Chodendo : the Japanese superconductivity
business / by Herbert Glazer.
Tokyo : Sophia University, 1989.
HD9696.S963J34 1989

[D]Golovashkin, A.I.
Fizicheskie proëtìsessy v sverkhprovodëìiashchikh
ustroæistvakh / otvetstvennyæi redaktor toma, A.I.
Golovashkin.
Moskva : "Nauka", 1991.
QC1.A4 t. 205; Alternative class.: QC761.3

[D]Goodrich, L.F.
Critical current measurements on an NbTi
superconducting wire standard reference material / L.F.
Goodrich ... [et al.].
Gaithersburg, MD : U.S. Dept. of Commerce,
National Bureau of Standards ; Washington, DC : For sale by
the Supt. of Docs., U.S. G.P.O., 1984.
QC100.U57 no. 260-91; Alternative class.:
TK7872.S8

[D]Grant, Paul M.; Researchers find extraordinarily high temperature superconductivity in bio-inspired nanopolymer; Physics Today.v. 51 no5 May '98 p. 17-19.
One of three winning essays of the Physics Tomorrow essay contest is presented. Scientists have announced the discovery of superconductivity at more than 600 K in a laboratory-created, computationally designed polymer with structural properties similar to DNA. It is widely thought that the discovery could have a serious impact on the future course of global energy development.

[D]Greenberg, Ya. S.; Application of superconducting quantum interference devices to nuclear magnetic resonance; Reviews of Modern Physics.v. 70 Jan. '98 p. 175-222.
The author outlines the experimental and theoretical studies in which superconducting quantum interference devices (SQUIDs) have been implemented in the detection of NMR. Special attention is given to the computation of the signal-to-noise ratio of SQUID NMR spectrometers with various input configurations as compared to that of conventional ones. The use of SQUIDs in nuclear thermometry and in absolute field measurements is considered, and the longitudinal nuclear magnetization is discussed in detail.

[D]Gregory, W. D. , W. N. Mathews, Jr., and E. A. Edelsack (eds.)
The Science and technology of superconductivity.
New York, Plenum Press, 1973.
TK7872.S8S34

[D]H.-U. Haberheier, M.L. Hitchman
Symposium F on High Temperature Superconductor
Thin Films: Growth Mechanisms-Interfaces-Multilayers (1996 :
Strasbourg, France)
High temperature superconductor thin
films--growth mechanisms-interfaces-multilayers : proceedings
of Symposium F on High Temperature Superconductor Thin
Films--Growth Mechanisms-Interfaces-Multilayers of the 1996
E-MRS Spring Conference, Strasbourg, France, June 4-7, 1996 /
edited by H.-U. Haberheier, M.L. Hitchman.
Amsterdam ; New York : Elsevier, c1997.
QC176.82.S883 1997

[D]H.-Ulrich Wienands
The SSC low energy booster : design and component
prototypes for the first injector synchrotron / edited by
H.-Ulrich Wienands ; contributing authors, R. Aiello ... [et. al.].
New York : IEEE Press, c1997.
QC787.P7S85 1997

[D]Hale, Phyllis
Supercollider 5 / edited by Phyllis Hale.
New York : Plenum Press, c1994.
QC787.P7S8668 1994

[D]Harold Weinstock, Martin Nisenoff
NATO Advanced Study Institute on Superconducting
Electronics (1988 : Il Ciocco, Italy)
Superconducting electronics / edited by Harold
Weinstock, Martin Nisenoff.
Berlin ; New York : Springer-Verlag, c1989.
TK7872.S8N23 1988

[D]Haruyama, T.
Pressure drop in forced two phase cooling of the
large thin superconducting solenoid / T. Haruyama ... [et al.].
Ibaraki-ken, Japan : National Laboratory for High
Energy Physics, 1987.

[D]Hein, Matthias, 1961-
High-temperature superconducting thin films at
microwave frequencies / Matthias Hein.

New York : Springer, 1999.
QC1.S797 vol. 155; Alternative class.:
QC611.98.H54

[D]Heinen, Vernon O. , Kul B. Bhasin
Superconductivity applications for infrared and
microwave devices II : 4-5 April 1991, Orlando, Florida /
; sponsoredand published by SPIE--the International Society for Optical Engineering ;
cooperating organization, CREOL/University of Central Florida.
Bellingham, Wash. : SPIE, c1991.
TK7872.T55S850 1991

[D]Hines, Jennifer.
Siting the Superconducting Super Collider in
Northeastern Illinois : environmental screening atlas /
Jennifer K. Hines ; with contributions by Illinois State
Geological Survey ... [et al.].
Springfield : Illinois Dept. of Energy and
Natural Resources, 1986.
G1409.B2N35H5 1986

[D]Hinken, Johann H., 1946-
Supraleiter-Elektronik. English
Superconductor electronics : fundamentals and
microwave applications / Johann H. Hinken ; [translator, A.H.
Armstrong].
Berlin ; New York : Springer-Verlag, c1989.
TK7872.S8H5613 1989

[D]IEEE transactions on applied superconductivity :
a publication of the IEEE Superconductivity Committee.
New York, NY : Institute of Electrical and
Electronics Engineers, c1991-
TK7872.S8I35

[D]Il'ichev, V. I.
Vysokotemperaturnaëìia sverkhprovodimost',
keramicheskikh sistem / V.I. Il'ichev, M.A. Savchenko, A.V.
Stefanovich.
Moskva : Nauka, 1992.
QC611.98.H54I44 1992

[D]International Conference on Magnet Technology,
3d, Hamburg, 1970.
Proceedings, ed. by Ed. Comm. MT3. Organized by
Dt. Elektronen-Synchrotron, DESY, Hamburg.

Hamburg, DESY, 1970.
TK454.4.E5I57 1970

[D]International Symposium on New Developments in
Applied Superconductivity (1988 : Suita-shi, Japan)
International Symposium on New Developments in
Applied Superconductivity : Suita, Osaka, Japan, 17-19 Oct.
1988 : a supplement of annual report of Laboratory for
Applied Superconductivity, Osaka University / editor, Y. Murakami.
Singapore ; Teaneck, NJ : World Scientific, c1989.
TK7872.S8I5775 1988

[D]Investigation of superconducting pulse magnets
for energy storage : final report / Kauppinen Ossi ... [et al.].
Tampere : Tampere University of Technology, Lab.
of Electricity and Magnetism, 1987.
TK2985.I58 1987

[D]Iwasa, Yukikazu.
Case studies in superconducting magnets : design
and operational issues / Yukikazu Iwasa.
New York : Plenum Press, c1994.
QC761.3.I9 1994

[D]J. Brau, R.S.Panvini.
International Conference on High Energy Physics
(8th : 1987 : Vanderbilt University)
Collider physics : current status and future
prospects : 8th International Conference on High Energy
Physics at Vanderbilt, Vanderbilt University, Nashville,
Tennessee, 8-10 October 1987 / editors, J. Brau, R.S. Panvini.
Singapore ; New York : World Scientific, 1988.
QC793.I553 1987

[D]Jha, A. R.
Superconductor technology : applications to
microwave, electro-optics, electrical machines, and
propulsion sytems / A.R. Jha.
New York : Wiley, c1998.
TK454.4.S93J43 1998

[D]Kadin, Alan M.
Introduction to superconducting circuits / Alan M. Kadin.
New York : Wiley, c1999.
TK7872.S8K26 1999

[D]Kao , Yi-Han, Philip Coppens & Hoi-Sing Kwok.
Superconductivity and its applications, Buffalo, NY, 1990
New York : American Institute of Physics, 1991.
QC611.9.S854 1991

[D]Kao, Y.H. , A.E. Kaloyeros & H.S. Kwok.
Superconductivity and its applications : Buffalo, NY 1991,
New York : American Institute of Physics, c1992.
QC611.9.S855 1991

[D]Kelly, J.P. , M.J.Superczynski
American Society of Mechanical Engineers. Winter
Meeting (1992 : Anaheim, Calif.)
Heat transfer and superconducting magnetic energy
storage : presented at the Winter Annual Meeting of the
American Society of Mechanical Engineers, Anaheim,
California, November 8-13, 1992 / sponsored by the Heat
Transfer Division, ASME ; edited by J.P. Kelly, M.J. Superczynski.
New York : The Society, c1992.
TJ260.A415 1992

[D]Kempton, J.P.
Geological-geotechnical studies for siting the
superconducting super collider in Illinois : results of the
spring 1985 test drilling program / J.P. Kempton ... [et al.].
Champaign, Ill. (615 E. Peabody Drive, Champaign
61820) : Illinois State Geological Survey, 1987.
QE105.A32 no. 120; Alternative class.: QE106.B37

[D]Koyama, Ken-ichi, 1938-
Theoretical and experimental studies on magnetic
instability in a hard superconductor / Ken-ichi Koyama.
Tokyo : Electrotechnical Laboratory, 1973.
TK4.D33 no. 741; Alternative class.: QC612.S8

[D]Krech, W. , P. Seidel, H.-G. Meyer. (eds.)
Symposium on Superconductivity and
Cryoelectronics (22nd : 1990 : Georgenthal, Germany)
Superconductivity and cryoelectronics :
proceedings of the 22nd Symposium on Superconductivity and
Cryoelectronics /
Singapore ; River Edge, NJ : World Scientific, c1991.
QC611.9.S95 1990

[D]Krisch, A.D., & A.M.T. Lin, O. Chamberlain
Polarized beams at SSC, Ann Arbor, MI, 1985 ;
Polarized antiprotons, Bodega Bay, CA, 1985 / editors, A.D. Krisch & A.M.T. Lin, O. Chamberlain.
New York : American Institute of Physics, 1986.
QC793.3.B4P65 1986

[D]Kunze, Ulrich.
Quanteninterferenz-Feldeffekttransistoren,
Bauelemente für die Nanometer-Integration? / von Ulrich Kunze.
Mainz : Akademie der Wissenschaften und der Literatur ; Stuttgart : F. Steiner Verlag Wiesbaden, c1987.
Q49.M22 1987, Nr. 3; Alternative class.:
TK7871.95

[D]Kustom, Robert L.
Thyristor networks for the transfer of energy between superconducting coils / Robert L. Kustom.
Madison : University of Wisconsin Press, 1980.
TK2985.K87

[D]Kwok, Hoi S. and David T. Shaw
Conference on Superconductivity and Applications (2nd : 1988 : Buffalo, N.Y.)
Superconductivity and its applications :
proceedings of the Second Annual Conference on Superconductivity and Applications, held April 18-20, 1988, at the Buffalo Hyatt Regency Hotel, Buffalo, New York, USA /
New York : Elsevier, c1988.
QC611.9.C66 1988

[D]Kwok, Hoi S., David T. Shaw, Michael J. Naughton
Superconductivity and its applications : Buffalo, NY 1992, New York, NY : American Institute of Physics, c1993.
QC611.9.S855 1993

[D]Kwok, Hoi S., Yi-Han Kao, David T. Shaw
Conference on Superconductivity and Applications (3rd : 1989 : Buffalo, N.Y.)
Superconductivity and applications / edited by
New York : Plenum Press, c1989.
QC611.9.C66 1989

[D]L.Correra
Symposium A1 on High Temperature Superconductor Thin Films (1991 : Strasbourg, France)

High Tc superconductor thin films : proceedings
of Symposium A1 on High Temperature Superconductor Thin Films
of the International Conference on Advanced Materials--ICAM
91, Strasbourg, France, 27-31 May, 1991 / edited by L. Correra.
Amsterdam ; New York : North Holland ; New York,
N.Y., U.S.A. : Distributors for the United States and Canada,
Elsevier Science Pub. Co., 1992.
QC176.82.S88 1991

[D]Larbalestier, David, reviewer; Handbook of applied superconductivity (book review); Nature.v. 395 no6703 Oct. 15 '98 p. 657-8.

[D]Likharev, K. K. (Konstantin Konstantinovich)
Vvedenie v dinamiku dzhozefsonovskikh perekhodov
/ K.K. Likharev.
Moskva : "Nauka," Glav. red.
fiziko-matematicheskoæi lit-ry, 1985.
QC176.8.T8L56 1985

[D]Listing of superconducting websites
Address: http://www.cm.utexas.edu/mcdevitt/Links/Superconductor.html
American Superconductor; (magnet manufacturers;) ; Ames Research Lab; (Superconductivity research;); Applied Physics Systems (Magnetometer manufacturer); Applied Superconductivity Center at the University of Wisconsin-Madison;; Applied Superconductivity Lab at Saga University Brock University; (Superconductivity research); Can Superconductors; (Bismuth based products including demo kits, current leads and magnetic shielding;) Center for High Temperature Superconductivity at the Imperial College in London, England; Clark University; Organic Superconductor Research; Colorado Superconductor Educational Superconductor Kits; Conductus, Inc; High-Tc electronics manufacturer; Cryomagnetics magnets and cryostats manufacturer; Dr; John T; McDevitt's research group at the University of Texas at Austin; Dr; Tinkham's research group at Harvard; European Superconductor Supply, Limited; Research, development and manufacture of superconducting materials; EURUS Technologies; YBCO based current leads, BSCCO tapes, bonding alloys; Everson Electric Company Superconductor magnet producer; High-Tc Update; Superconductor newsletter; Hypres, Inc; Superconducting Electronics Company Illinois Superconductor wireless communication company; IRC; Interdisciplinary Research Center in Superconductivity at the University of Cambridge; Korea Research Institute Superconductivity Group; Laboratory for Applied Superconductivity and Magnetism Ohio State University; National Superconducting Cyclotron Lab at Michigan State University; MITER Magnetic and Superconducting Materials in Italy; Oak Ridge National Lab High Tc materials; Oak Ridge National Lab; Computational studies on YBCO; Pohang Superconductivity Center in Korea; Quantum Design magnetometer manufacturer; Science and Technology Center for Superconductivity; UIUC, Illinois Sixth International Conference on Materials and Mechanisms of Superconductivity and

High Temperature Superconductors held in Houston, Texas, from February 20 to February 25, 2000; Superconducting Detector Research at the University of London; Superconducting ceramics at the Centre for Microscopy and Microanalysis at the University of Queensland; Superconducting Core Technologies RF wireless company; Superconducting Super Collider Project Now defunct;; Superconductivity for Electric Systems DOE supported; Superconductor Week Newsletter of Record in Superconductor Industry SUPRAS at the University of Liege, Belgium; TCSUH; Texas Center for Superconductivity at the University of Houston; Texas Materials Institute at the University of Texas at Austin; University of Maryland; Center for Superconductivity Research University of Rochester; Superconducting Digital Electronics Yoichi Okabe; Superconductive Electronics Research

[D]Listing of superconducting websites.
Address: http://physics.sogang.ac.kr/~super/super/link.html
This site contains a List of Other Superconductivity Web Sites including Korean Laboratories ; Japanese Laboratories ; UK Superconductivity Research US Government Organizations and FFRDCs ; US Industrial Organizations ; US Universities ; Other Universities ; Other Conferences with Sessions on Applied Superconductivity

[D]M.P. Mattis and E. Mottola
Baryon number violation at the SSC? : proceedings of the Santa Fe workshop, 27-30 April 1990 / M.P. Mattis and E. Mottola.[SUPERCOLLIDER]
Singapore ; Teaneck, NJ : World Scientific Pub. Co., 1990.
QC793.5.B32B37 1990

[D]Marinucci, C. , P. Weymuth
International Conference on Magnet Technology (9th : 1985 : Zurich, Switzerland)
Proceedings of the 9th International Conference on Magnet Technology, Zurich (Switzerland), September 9-13, 1985 / editors, C. Marinucci, P. Weymuth ; organized by Swiss Institute for Nuclear Research (SIN) at the Swiss Federal Institute of Technology (ETH).
Villigen, Switzerland : SIN, [1985]
QC756.7.I57 1985

[D]Marner, W. J.,
American Society of Mechanical Engineers. Winter Meeting (1989 : San Francisco, Calif.)
Collected papers in heat transfer, 1989 :
presented at the Winter Annual Meeting of the American Society of Mechanical Engineers, San Francisco, California, December 10-15, 1989 / sponsored by the Heat Transfer

Division ; edited by W. J. Marner, ... [et. al.].
New York, N.Y. : American Society of Mechanical Engineers, c1989.
TJ260.A415 1989c

[D]Martini, F.De, G. Denardo, A. Zeilinger
Adriatico Workshop on Quantum Interferometry (1993 : Trieste, Italy)
Proceedings of the Adriatico Workshop on Quantum Interferometry : 2-5 March 1993, Trieste, Italy / editors F. De Martini, G. Denardo, A. Zeilinger.
Singapore ; River Edge, NJ : World Scientific, c1994.
QC410.9.A37 1993

[D]May, Mike; All together now; New Scientist.v. 155 Sept. 20 '97 p. 16.
U.S. scientists have developed an operating system for a computer no one yet knows how to build that performs 1,000 trillion floating point operations per second. The scientists believe that the key is what they call a hybrid multithreaded (HMT) design. The computer would have 4,000 parallel superconducting processors provided with data by superconducting memory chips. An HMT machine would have as many as 128 queues at every processor, each one dealt with in turn. Preparation units would examine the instructions at the front of each queue, determine what data the processor will need to execute them, and put the necessary data into the superconducting memory near the processor.

[D]Mayo, Jonathan L.
Superconductivity : the threshold of a new technology / Jonathan L. Mayo.
Blue Ridge Summit, PA : Tab Books, c1988.
QC612.S8M39 1988

[D]McAshan, Michael
International Industrial Symposium on the Supercollider (1st : 1989 : New Orleans, La.)
Supercollider 1 / edited by Michael McAshan.
New York : Plenum Press, c1989.
QC787.P7I57 1989

[D]McAshan, Michael
International Industrial Symposium on the Supercollider (2nd : 1990 : Miami Beach, Fla.)
Supercollider 2 / edited by Michael McAshan.
New York : Plenum Press, c1990.
QC787.P7I57 1990

[D]McKay, J.W.
Symposium of Northeastern Accelerator Personnel
(1992 : Hull, Quebec and Chalk River, Ontario)
Symposium of North Eastern Accelerator Personnel
Hull, Quebec, and Chalk River, Ontario, AECL Research,
Chalk River Laboratories, September 23-25, 1992 / editor,
J.W. McKay.
Singapore ; New Jersey : World Scientific, c1995.
QC787.P3S956 1992

[D]Melvin Month, Per F. Dahl, and Margaret Dienes
Summer School on High Energy Particle
Accelerators (3rd : 1983 : Brookhaven National Laboratory and
State University of New York at Stony Brook)
The state of high energy physics / BNL/SUNY
Summer School, 1983 ; edited by Melvin Month, Per F. Dahl,
and Margaret Dienes.
New York : American Institute of Physics, 1985.
QC793.S87 1983

[D]Mess, K.-H.
Superconducting accelerator magnets / K.-H. Mess,
P. Schmüser, S. Wolff.
Singapore ; River Edge, NJ : World Scientific, c1996.
QC761.3.M47 1996

[D]Meyerhoff, Robert W.
Manufacture of superconducting materials :
proceedings of an international conference, 8-10 November
1976, Port Chester, New York / sponsored by the Hudson Valley
Chapter and Technical Divisions and Activities, American
Society for Metals ; edited by Robert W. Meyerhoff.
Metals Park, Ohio : American Society for Metals, c1977.
TS371.M36

[D]Michigan. Superconducting Super Collider Commission.
Siting the Superconducting Super Collider in
Michigan : a report to the Governor, the Legislature, the
People of Michigan / by the Michigan Superconducting Super
Collider Commission.
[Lansing]: The Commission, [1989]
QC787.P7M53 1989

[D]Microwave Studies of High Temperature Superconductors. Part I. (Volume 17 -
Studies of High Temperature Superconductors)
Anant Narlikar (Editor)
1996, 262 pages. ISBN 1-56072-380-7. $110

Contents: Chapter 1 - Field Modulated Microwave Absorption, Harmonic Generation and Magnetic Properties of YBa2Cu3O7 Thin Films (J. Dumas, C. Schlenker, B.P. Thrane, A. Neminsky): Chapter 2 - Magnetic Field Induced Microwave Losses in High-Tc Superconductors (M. Mahei); Chapter 3 -; Microwave Magneto Absorption in High Temperature Superconductors (S. M. Bhagat, S. Tyagi); Chapter 4 - Microwave Dissipation in High-Tc Superconductors in a Magnetic Field; (R. Fastampa, M. Giura, R. Marcon, E. Silva); Chapter 5 - Microwave Surface Resistance of High Tc Superconducting Films(R. Pinto); Chapter 6 - Surface Resistance Measurement Techniques (A. P. Jenkins, K. S. Kale, D. Dew-Hughes); Chapter 7 - Microwave Penetration Depth Measurement in High-Tc Superconductors (A. P. Mourachkine, R. F. Barel)

[D]Microwave Studies of High Temperature Superconductors. Part II. (Volume 18 - Studies of High Temperature Superconductors)
Anant Narlikar (Ed.)
1996, 271 pages. ISBN 1-56072-381-5. $110
Contents: Chapter 1 - Radio-Frequency Investigations of High-Temperature Superconductors (A. Pimenov, P. Lunkenhiemer, M. Dressel, G. Knebel,A. Loidl); Chapter 2. Microwave Surface Impedance of High Temperature Superconductors and Device Applications (N. D. Kataria, M. Jaya Kumar, G. P. Srivastava); Chapter 3 - Microwave Study of the Mixed State and Superconducting Fluctuations in YBa2Cu3O7 Single Crystals (A. Dulcic, M Pozek, I. Ukrainczyk); Chapter 4 - Microwave Properties of High-Temperature Superconductors; Surface Impedance, Circuits and Systems (Matthias A. Hein); Chapter 5 - Zero-Field and Magnetic Field Dependent Microwave and Radio Frequency Absorption in the High Temperature Superconductors (F. J. Owens, Z. Iqbal); Chapter 6 - Anomalous Low-Magnetic-Field Dependence of Non-Resonant Microwave and RF Absorption in High-Tc Superconductors (S V Bhat)

[D]Mikhailov, G. A.
Krioçelektronnye komponenty çEVM : [Sb. stateæi]
/ AN USSR, Nauch. sovet po probl. Kibernetika, In-t
kibernetiki ; [Otv. red. G. A. Mikhailov].
Kiev : IK, 1977.
TK7895.C7K74

[D]Miller, Richard Kendall, 1946-
Survey on high-Tc superconductor applications /
by Richard K. Miller.
Madison, GA : Future Technology Surveys, [c1989]
HD9696.S963U65 1989

[D]Miller, Richard Kendall, 1946-
Survey on SQUID sensors / by Richard K. Miller and Terri C. Walker.
Madison, GA : Future Technology Surveys, c1989.
HD9696.S963U652 1989

[D]Miller, Richard Kendall, 1946-
Survey on superconductor magnetic energy storage
by Richard K. Miller and Terri C. Walker.
Madison, GA : Future Technology Surveys,
[c1989].
HD9696.S962M55 1989

[D]Montgomery, D. Bruce (Donald Bruce), 1933-
Solenoid magnet design; the magnetic and
mechanical aspects of resistive and superconducting systems
[by]D. Bruce Montgomery.
New York, Wiley-Interscience [1969]
TK2391.M66

[D]Montgomery, D. Bruce (Donald Bruce), 1933-
Solenoid magnet design : the magnetic and
mechanical aspects of resistive and superconducting systems /
D. Bruce Montgomery, with the assistance of Robert J.
Weggel.
Huntington, N.Y. : R. E. Krieger Pub. Co., 1979, c1969.
TK2391.M66 1980

[D]Moon, F. C., 1939-
Superconducting levitation : applications to
bearings and magnetic transportation / Francis C. Moon ; with
selected sections by Pei-Zen Chang.
New York : Wiley, c1994.
QC611.98.H54M66 1994

[D]Morpurgo, Mario.
Construction of a superconducting test coil
cooled by Helium forced circulation, [by]M. Morpurgo.
Geneva, CERN, 1968.
QC770.E8 1968, no. 17

[D]Nakano, Hiroshi.
DC-SQUIDs fabricated by shapes of sputtering
deposition at step edge and anodic oxidization / by Hiroshi
Nakano and Takafumi Aomine.
Fukuoka, Japan : [Kyushu University Research
Institute of Fundamental Information Science, 1986]
TK7872.S8N17 1986

[D]Newhouse, Vernon L.
Applied superconductivity, by Vernon L. Newhouse.
New York, Wiley [1964]
TK7872.S8N4

[D]Newhouse, Vernon L.
Applied superconductivity, edited by Vernon L. Newhouse.
New York, Academic Press, 1975.
TK7872.S8N42

[D]Newton, David E.
Particle accelerators : from the cyclotron to the superconducting super collider / David E. Newton.
New York : F. Watts, 1989.
QC787.P3N48 1989

[D]Niobium and niobium alloys : superconducting applications.
Warrendale, Pa. : Minerals, Metals and Materials Soc., 1989.

[D]Nonte, John
International Industrial Symposium on the Supercollider (3rd : 1991 : Atlanta, Ga.)
Supercollider 3 / edited by John Nonte.
New York : Plenum, c1991.
QC787.P7I57 1991

[D]Nonte, John
Supercollider 4 / edited by John Nonte.
New York : Plenum Press, c1992.
QC787.P7S8667 1992

[D]Norman, Scott L., 1940-
Far-infrared absorption spectra of thick superconducting films [microform]. 1968.
Microfilm 20812

[D]Northern Great Plains superconducting super collider site proposal / submitted by State of South Dakota, Office of the Governor.
Pierre, SD : The Office, [1987]
QC787.P7N67 1987

[D]Opportunities in superconductivity applications.
New York, N.Y. (106 Fulton St., New York 10038) :
Frost & Sullivan, c1989.
HD9696.S963U66 1989

[D]Opportunities in superconductivity applications.
New York, N.Y. (106 Fulton St., New York 10038) :
Frost & Sullivan, c1989.
HD9696.S963U66 1989

[D]Orlando, Terry P.
Foundations of applied superconductivity / Terry P. Orlando, Kevin A. Delin.
Reading, Mass. : Addison-Wesley, c1991.
QC611.92.O75 1990

[D]Otala, Matti.
The theory and construction of a proposed superconducting aeromagnetic gradiometer.
Helsinki [Finnish Academy of Technical Sciences] 1969.
TK4.A26 no. 21

[D]Out of control : lessons learned from the Superconducting Super Collider : a staff report / prepared for the use of the Subcommittee on Oversight and Investigations of the Committee on Energy and Commerce, U.S. House of Representatives.
Washington : U.S. G.P.O. : For sale by the U.S. G.P.O., Supt. of Docs., Congressional Sales Office, 1995.
QC787.P73O97 1995

[D]Owens, Frank J.
The new superconductors / Frank J. Owens and Charles P. Poole, Jr.
New York : Plenum Press, c1996.
QC611.95.O89 1996

[D]Ozaki, S. , S. Kurokawa, Y. Unno
ICFA Seminar on "Future Perspectives in High Energy Physics" (1984 : K¯o-enerug¯i Butsurigaku Kenky¯ujo)
Proceedings of the 1984 ICFA Seminar on "Future Perspectives in High Energy Physics," May 14-20, 1984, KEK / edited by S. Ozaki, S. Kurokawa, Y. Unno.
¯Oh¯o-machi, Tsukuba-gun, Ibaraki-ken, Japan : National Laboratory for High Energy Physics, c1984.
QC787.P7I24 1984

[D]Padamsee, Hasan, 1945-
RF superconductivity for accelerators / Hasan Padamsee, Jens Knobloch, Tom Hays.
New York : Wiley, c1998.
QC787.P3P33 1998

[D]Palmer, D.N.(ed.)
Superconductivity advances and applications, 1989 : presented at the Winter Annual Meeting of the American

Society of Mechanical Engineers, San Francisco, California,
December 10-15, 1989 / sponsored by the Superconductivity
Technical Committee of the Advanced Energy Systems Division,
ASME ; New York, N.Y. : ASME, c1989.
QP82.2.M3S86 1989

[D]Parsch, Claus Peter.
Supraleiter und supraleitende Magnete / von Claus
Peter Parsch.
Berlin ; München : Siemens-Aktiengesellschaft,
[Abt. Verl.], 1975.
QC761.3.P37

[D]Pavuna, Davor ,Ivan Bozovic
Oxide superconductor physics and nano-engineering
: 26-28 January 1994, Los Angeles, California / Davor Pavuna,
Ivan Bozovic, chairs/editors ; sponsored and published by
SPIE--the International Society for Optical Engineering.
Bellingham, Wash., USA : SPIE, c1994.
QC611.98.H54O95 1994

[D]Pavuna, Davor Ivan Bozovic
Superconducting and related oxides, physics and
nanoengineering III : 20-24 July, 1998, San Diego, California
/ Davor Pavuna, Ivan Bozovic, chairs/editors ; sponsored by
SPIE--the International Society for Optical Engineering ;
cosponsored by Oxxel GmbH Bremen, (Germany) ; published by
SPIE--The International Society for Optical Engineering.
Bellingham, Wash. : SPIE, c1998.
QC611.98.H54S86 1998

[D]Poitevin, C.
Proceedings of the second workshop, non tidal
gravity changes : intercomparison between absolute and
superconducting gravimeters : September 6th to 8th, 1994,
Walferdange (Grand-Duchy of Luxemburg) / organized by the
IAG, International Gravity Commission-Working Group V,
Monitoring of Non Tidal Gravity Variations and the European
Centre for Geodynamics and Seismology (EUR-OPA Major Hazards)
edited by C. Poitevin.
Luxembourg : Centre Européen de Géodynamique et de Séismologie, 1995.
QB330.P764 1995

[D]Poitevin, C.
Proceedings of the workschop [i.e. workshop], non
tidal gravity changes : intercomparison between absolute and
superconducting gravimeters : September 5th to 7th, 1990,

Walferdange (Grand-Duchy of Luxemburg) / organized by the European Centre for Geodynamics and [i.e. and]Seismology (Council of Europe) and the IAG-International Gravity Commission-Working Group V, Monitoring of Non Tidal Gravity Variations ; edited by C. Poitevin.
Luxembourg : Centre européen de géodynamique et de séismologie, Musée d'histoire naturelle, Section astrophysique et géophysique, 1991.
QB330.P77 1991

[D]Processing of films for high Tc superconducting electronics : 10-12 October 1989, Santa Clara, California / T. Venkatesan, chair/editor ; sponsored by SPIE--The International Society for Optical Engineering ; cooperating organizations, Center for Advanced Electronic Materials Processing/North Carolina State University, Engineering Research Center for Plasma-Aided Manufacturing/University of Wisconsin-Madison, SEMATECH.
Bellingham, Wash., USA : SPIE, c1990.
TK7872.T55P76 1990

[D]Projects on "High temperature superconductivity"
Azerbaijan, Armenia, Estonia, Byelorussia, Russia, Ukraine.
Moscow : International Centre for Scientific and Technical Information, 1992.
QC611.98.H54P77 1992

[D]Reed,M.A...
Nanostructure physics and fabrication :
proceedings of the international symposium, College Station, Texas, March 13-15, 1989 / edited by Mark A. Reed, Wiley P. Kirk.
Boston : Academic Press, c1989.
QC176.8.E4N32 1989

[D]Rene Donaldson and Jorge G. Morfín
Summer Study on the Design and Utilization of the Superconducting Super Collider (1984 : Snowmass, Colo.)
Proceedings of the 1984 Summer Study on the Design and Utilization of the Superconducting Super Collider, June 23-July 13, 1984, Snowmass, Colorado / editors, Rene Donaldson and Jorge G. Morfín ; organized by the Division of Particles and Fields of the American Physical Society ; sponsored jointly by the Division of Particles and Fields of the American Physical Society ... [et al.].
[New York, N.Y.]: The Division, 1984.
QC787.P7S86 1984

[D]Rene Donaldson and M.G.D. Gilchriese
Workshop on Calorimetry for the Superconducting Supercollider (1989 : Tuscaloosa (Ala.)
Proceedings of the workshop on Calorimetry for the Superconducting Supercollider, University of Alabama, Tuscaloosa, Alabama, March 13-17, 1989 / Rene Donaldson and M.G.D. Gilchriese, editors.
Singapore : Teaneck, N.J. : World Scientific, 1990.
QC787.P7W66 1989

[D]Roger L. Stockbauer, S.V. Krishnaswamy, Richard L.Kurtz
High TC superconducting thin films : processing, characterization, and applications, Boston, MA 1989 / editors, Roger L. Stockbauer, S.V. Krishnaswamy, Richard L. Kurtz.
New York : American Institute of Physics, c1990.
TK7871.15.F5H54 1990

[D]Ruggiero, Alessandro G.
INFN ELOISATRON Project. Workshop (34th : 1996 : Erice, Italy)
Hadron colliders at the highest energy and luminosity : proceedings of the 34th Workshop of the INFN Elosiatron Project : Erice, Italy, 4-13 November 1996 / editor, Alessandro G. Ruggiero.
Singapore ; New Jersey : World Scientific, c1998.
QC787.C59I53 1996

[D]S. Shlomo, R.P. Schmitt, J.B. Natowitz
Texas A & M Symposium on Hot Nuclei (1987 : College Station, Tex.)
Proceedings of the Texas A&M Symposium on Hot Nuclei : organized on the occasion of the dedication of the Texas A&M Superconducting K500 Cyclotron, College Station, Texas, December 7-10, 1987 / editors, S. Shlomo, R.P. Schmitt, J.B. Natowitz.
Singapore ; Teaneck, N.J. : World Scientific, 1988.
QC794.8.H4T49 1987

[D]S.N. Erné, H.-D. Hahlbohm, H. Lübbig
International Workshop on Biomagnetism (3rd : 1980 : Berlin, Germany)
Biomagnetism : proceedings, third International Workshop on Biomagnetism, Berlin (West), May 1980 / editors, S.N. Erné, H.-D. Hahlbohm, H. Lübbig.
Berlin ; New York : De Gruyter, 1981.
QP345.I57 1980

[D]Sacchetti, N. , M. Spadoni, S. Stipcich
International Conference on Magnet Technology,
5th, Rome, 1975.
Proceedings / Fifth International Conference on
Magnet Technology (MT-5) Roma (EUR), Italy, April 21-25, 1975
; edited by N. Sacchetti, M. Spadoni, S. Stipcich ; organized
by Laboratori nazionali del CNEN, Frascati.
Frascati : Laboratori nazionali del CNEN,
Servizio documentazione, 1975.
TK454.4.E5I57 1975

[D]Sanford, James R.
International Conference on High Energy Physics
(26th : 1992 : Dallas, Tex.)
Proceedings of the XXVI International Conference
on High Energy Physics : August 6-12, 1992, Dallas, Texas /
editor James R. Sanford ; sponsored by the Superconducting
Super Collider Laboratory [and]Universities Research
Association, Inc.
New York, NY : American Institute of Physics, c1993.
QC793.I553 1992

[D]Savchenko, M. A.
Fluktuaëtìsionnaëïìa sverkhprovodimost'
magnitnykh sistem / M.S. Savchenko, A.V. Stefanovich ;
otvetstvennyæi redaktor U.Kh. Kopvillem.
Moskva : "Nauka", 1986.
QC761.3.S28 1986

[D]Schoenung, S.M. (ed.)
American Society of Mechanical Engineers. Winter
Meeting (1988 : Chicago, Ill.)
Superconductivity applications and developments :
presented at the Winter Annual Meeting of the American
Society of Mechanical Engineers, Chicago, Illinois, November
27-December 2, 1988 / sponsored by the Materials Division, ASME
New York, N.Y. (345 E. 47th St., New York 10017) : ASME, c1988.
QC611.9.A44 1988

[D]Schwartz, Brian B., and Simon Foner
Nato Advanced Study Institute on Small-Scale
Applications of Superconductivity, Gardone Riviera, Italy, 1976.
Superconductor applications : SQUIDs and machines
/ edited by Brian B. Schwartz and Simon Foner.
New York : Plenum Press, c1977.
TK7872.S8N2 1976

[D]Sekiguchi, T. and S. Shimamoto
International Conference on Magnet Technology
(11th : 1989 : Tsukuba, Japan)
11th International Conference on Magnet
Technology (MT-11) / edited by T. Sekiguchi and S. Shimamoto
MT-11, Tsukuba, Japan ; The Institute of Electrical
Engineers of Japan.
London ; New York : Elsevier Applied Science ;
New York, NY, USA : Sole distributor in the U.S. and Canada,
Elsevier Science Pub. Co., c1990.
QC756.7I57 1989

[D]Selection and geology of Oklahoma's
Superconducting Super Collider site / Kenneth V. Luza ... [et al.].
Norman, Okla. : Oklahoma Geological Survey,
University of Oklahoma, 1989.
QE154.K56S45 1989

[D]Sheadhen, Thomas.
Industrial superconductivity : opportunities and
applications / Thomas Sheahen.
Lilburn, Ga. : The Fairmont Press, 1989.
8903 BOOK NOT YET IN LC

[D]Shen, Zhi-Yuan.
High-temperature superconducting microwave
circuits / Zhi-Yuan Shen.
Boston : Artech House, c1994.
TK7876.S52 1994

[D]Simultaneous Engineering Conference, June 8,
1989, Dearborn, Michigan ... : creative manufacturing
engineering program.
Dearborn, Mich. (1 SME Dr., Dearborn 48121) :
Society of Manufacturing Engineers, c1989.
TS176.S557 1989

[D]Site proposal for the Superconducting Super
Collider.
Raleigh, N.C. : Office of the Governor, State of
North Carolina, [1987]
QC787.P7S58 1987

[D]Solid-state electronics.
Oxford, New York, Pergamon Press.
TK7872.S4S546

[D]Soper, Davison E.
Oregon Workshop on Super High Energy Physics
(1985 : University of Oregon)
Supercollider physics : proceedings of the Oregon
Workshop on Super High Energy Physics / Davison E. Soper, editor.
Singapore ; [Philadelphia]: World Scientific, c1986.
QC787.P7O74 1985

[D]Steven T.Ruggiero, David A. Rudman
Superconducting devices / edited by Steven T.
Ruggiero, David A. Rudman.
Boston : Academic Press, c1990.
TK7872.S8S79 1990

[D]Stoffle, Richard W.
Social assessment of high technology : the
superconducting super collider in Southeast Michigan /
Richard W. Stoffle ... [et al.].
Ann Arbor, Mich. : Survey Research Center/Center
for Political Studies, Institute for Social Research,
University of Michigan, 1987.
QC787.P7S63 1987

[D]Stoffle, Richard W.
The Superconducting super collider at the
Stockbridge, Michigan, site : community support and land
acquisition / Richard W. Stoffle ... [et al.].
Ann Arbor, Mich. : Survey Research Center, Center
for Political Studies, Institute for Social Research,
University of Michigan, 1988.
QC787.P7S867 1988

[D]Stork, D..
Conference on Linear Collider B-B Factory
Conceptual Design (1987 : Los Angeles, Calif.)
Proceedings of the Conference on Linear Collider
B-B Factory Conceptual Design, Los Angeles, California, 26-30
Jan. 1987 / editor, D. Stork.
New Jersey : World Scientific, c1987.
QC793.5.M422C66 1987

[D]Studies of High Temperature Superconductors. Volume 12.
High Tc Squids and Related Studies
Anant Narlikar (Ed.)
212 pages. 1994. $125. ISBN 1-56072-184-7.
Superconductivity; Physics; Chemistry; Materials Science; Solid State
Contents: • Chapter-L: Squids Made Of High Tc Super-Conductors (Y.N. Polushkin And

H. Koch); • Chapter-2: High Tc Squids: A Review (A.K. Gupta And N. Khare); • Chapter-3: Progress In Thin Film High Tc Squid Magnetometers (V. Foglietti); • Chapter-4: Josephson Behaviour Of Artificial Grain Boundary Junctions Of Superconducting $YBa_2Cu_3O_7$ (Shiguang Wang); • Chapter-5: Noise Thermometry With High Temperature Superconducting Josephson Junctions (John Gallop); • Chapter-6: Properties And Aplications Of High Tc Thin Film Devices. (Ling Hao And J. C. Macfarlane); • Subject Index.

[D]Studies of High Temperature Superconductors. Volume 13. HTSC Thin Films
Anant Narlikar (Ed.)
323 Pages. 1994. $125. ISBN 1-56072-183-9.
Contents: • Chapter-1: Epitaxial Growth Of (Re)Bacuo Structural Characterization, Control And Mechanisms (A. Perrin, M. Guilloux-Viry, C. Thivet And M. Sergent); • Chapter-2: Preparation And Properties Of High Tc Tlcabacuo Superconducting Thin Films (W.Y. Lee; J.S. Martens; E.L. Venturini); • Chapter-3: Realization Of Epitaxial Growth Of High Tc Superconducting Films And Study Of Their Physical Properties (S.B. Ogale And S.M.Kanetkar); • Chapter-4: Advanced Technique Of Structure Control For Bisrcacuo Thin Films (I. Tsukada, H. Watanabe, I. Terasaki And K. Uchinokura); • Chapter-5: Microstructure And Properties Of High Tc Superconducting Thin Films As Revealed By Raman Micro-Spectroscopy (Pham V. Huong); • Chapter-6: Nature And Physics Of High Tc Superconducting Thin Films (Jacob Azoulay); • Chapter-7: Sputter Deposition Of Ybacuo Thin Films (S.C. Sabharwal, D.K. Aswal, A.K. Debnath And M.K. Gupta); • Chapter-8: Electrosynthesis Of Compound Layers Of High Tc Superconductors; (S.H. Pawar; V.N. Shinde; A.V. Narlikar); • Subject Index

[D]Studies of High Temperature Superconductors. Volume 15.
Electron Microscopy and Channeling Studies of High Temperature Superconductors
Anant Narlikar (Ed.)
1995. 315 pages. ISBN 1-56072-219-3. $110
The present volume, that is Volume 15 of the series "Studies" , focuses on the use of transmission electron microscopy technique in the study of high temperature superconductors. One chapter (the first chapter) is devoted to ion channeling technique which, like TEM, has emerged as a powerful tool to unfold the structural and microstructural effects in HTSCs. The book contains eight chapters describing studies on a host of high Tc systems, including various cuprates and also recently discovered high Tc oxycarbonates. The contributors are some of the most active researchers in the field, and it is hoped that their efforts, presented in this volume, will go a long way in elucidating the frontal issues pertaining to structural and microstructural aspects of high Tc materials.

[D]Suematsu, Y.
Handbook of superconductor lasers and photonics / Y. Suematsu.
New York, NY : Chapman & Hall, 1994
9403

[D]Superconducting Super Collider : Cedar Mountains
siting proposal / submitted to the U.S. Department of Energy,
Office of Energy Research, SSC Site Task Force, by the State
of Utah, September 2, 1987 ; [prepared for State of Utah,
Department of Community and Economic Development, Division of
Business and Economic Development, by Dames & Moore ... et al.].
[Salt Lake City]: The Division, [1987]
QC787.P7S87 1987

[D]Superconducting Super Collider : Ripple Valley
siting proposal / submitted to the U.S. Department of Energy,
Office of Energy Research, SSC Site Task Force, by the State
of Utah, September 2, 1987 ; [prepared for State of Utah,
Department of Community and Economic Development, Division of
Business and Economic Development, by Dames & Moore ... et al.].
[Salt Lake City]: The Division, [1987]
QC787.P7S88 1987

[D]Superconductive technology in review / compiled
and published by the Educational Technology Center, Illinois
Institute of Technology.
Chicago, Ill. : The Center, [1982-

[D]Superconductivity Suppliers
Address: http://keelynet.com/sources/supercon.htm
A list of superconductivity suppliers. Advanced Ceramics Inc., NJ, M, 609-397-2900, 609-397-2708 Alfa Aesar Johnson Matthes, MA, M, 800-343-0660, 508-521-6350 All-Chemie LTD, SC, M, 803-884-4400, 803-884-0560 Alloys International Inc., NY, W, 516-342-0043, 516-342-0051 Angstrom Sciences, PA, M, 412-462-2777, 412-462-2780 California Fine Wire Co., CA, W, 805-489-5144, 805-489-5352 Commercial Crystal Labs Inc., FL, M, 914-643-5959, 914-643-6058 ESDI Inc., NY, C, 516-563-8278, 516-563-8231 G & J Steel & Tubing Inc., NJ, W, 800-322-8823, 908-526-9487 G&S Titanium, OH, W, 800-860-0564, 330-262-1550 GE Co., CT, M, 800-626-2004 Grove Grundilling Inc., ME, W, 207-743-7051, 207-743-7083 Hitachi Cable America, NY, M, 800-394-0234, 914-993-0990 HITC Superconductors Inc., NJ, M, 609-397-2700, 609-397-2708 Hypres Inc., NY, M, 914-592-1190, 914-347-2239 IGC Advanced Superconductors Inc., CT, W, 203-753-5215, 203-753-2096 Innovare Inc., PA, M, 610-837-8830 Intermagnetics General Corp., NY, M, 518-786-1122 InterWire Group, NY, W, 800-799-4978, 914-273-6510 MolecuWire Corp., NJ, W, 908-938-9473, 908-938-3189 Omega Engiuneering Inc., CT, W, 800-826-6342, 203-359-7700 Oxford Superconducting Technology, NJ, W, 908-541-1300, 908-541-7769 Rea Engineeered Wire Products Inc., IN, W, 219-422-4252, 219-422-4246 SAES Getters USA Inc., CO, M, 719-576-3200, 719-576-5025 Satcon Technology Corp., MA, M, 800-663-4916, 617-661-3373 SonoTec Corp., NY, C, 917-795-2020, 914-795-2720 Superconductive Componenets, OH, M, 800-346-6567, 800-292-8654 Superconductor Tech Inc., CA, M, 805-683-8527, 805-683-8527 Superconix Inc., MN, M, 612-222-0046, 612-222-0049

Vacuumschmelze (Siemens), NJ, M, 908-494-3530, 908-603-5994 Watteredge Uniflex Inc., OH, W, 216-871-9215, 216-933-8248

[D]Superconductor & cryoelectronics.
San Francisco, CA : Westtech Market Information
Services, 1998-

[D]Superconductor science & technology.
[Bristol, UK]: IOP Publishing Ltd, [c1988-
QC611.9.S86

[D]Symposium on Superconductive Techniques for
Computing Systems (1960 : Washington, D.C.) Proceedings.
Washingon, Office of Naval Research, Dept. of the Navy, 1960.
TK7895.C7S9 1960

[D]Texas National Research Laboratory Commission / a
staff report to the Sunset Advisory Commission.
Austin, Tex. (P.O. Box 13066, Capitol Station,
Austin 78711) : Sunset Advisory Commission, [1990]
QC787.P7T49 1990

[D]Texas National Research Laboratory Commission,
Research and Education Support, Superconducting Super
Collider Laboratory.[SUPERCOLLIDER]
DeSoto, Tex. (1801 North Hampton Road, Suite 400,
DeSoto, Tex. 75115) : Texas National Research Laboratory
Commission, [1992]
QC787.P73T49 1992

[D]The Denali site / offered to the U.S. Department
of Energy by the state of Alaska.
[Fairbanks, Alaska : State of Alaska, Office of the Governor, 1987]
QC787.P7D46 1987

[D]The Super collider--opening new frontiers into
inner space [videorecording]/ Division of Public Affairs,
U.S. Dept. of Energy.
Washington, DC : The Division : Distributed by
National Audiovisual Center, 1988.

[D]Thome, Richard J.
MHD and fusion magnets : field and force design
concepts / Richard J. Thome, John M. Tarrh.
New York : Wiley, c1982.
QC761.3.T47 1982

[D]Tiernan, W. M.; A superconducting persistent current experiment for an undergraduate laboratory; American Journal of Physics.v. 65 Aug. '97 p. 778-84.
The practical implementation of a superconducting persistent current experiment for an undergraduate laboratory is described. Persistent current experiments on polycrystalline YBa2Cu3O7-d (YBCO) rings at various magnetic fields were performed using an exchange gas cryostat immersed in liquid nitrogen, a 12 mT variable magnet, a low cost Hall sensor, and basic electronic instrumentation. Experiments to measure the critical current density and lower critical field of the YBCO ring and to investigate qualitative differences between the Meissner and vortex state are described.

[D]Torelli, Gabriele
Seminar on New Techniques for Future Accelerators
(3rd : 1989 : Erice, Italy)
New techniques for future accelerators III :
high-intensity storage rings--status and prospects for
superconducting magnets / edited by Gabriele Torelli.
New York : Plenum Press, c1990.
QC761.3.S46 1989

[D]Tournier , R., and R. Suryanarayanan
ICMAS 90 (1990)
ICMAS 90, from modern superconductivity towards
applications : proceedings of the international conference /
sponsored by IITT-International.
Gournay-sur-Marne : IITT-International, [1992?]
TK7872.S8I26 1990

[D]Treva J. Gourlay and Jorge G. Morfín
Symposium on Particle Identification at High
Luminosity Hadron Colliders (1989 : Batavia, Ill.)
Proceedings of the Symposium on Particle
Identification at High Luminosity Hadron Colliders : April
5-7, 1989 / editors, Treva J. Gourlay and Jorge G. Morfín.
Batavia, Ill. : Fermi National Accelerator
Laboratory, [1989]
QC787.P73S95 1989

[D]Tunnelling Studies of High Temperature Superconductors (Volume 20: Studies of High Temperature Superconductors).
Anant Narlikar (Ed.)
1996. 239 pages. ISBN 1-56072-394-7. $110.
Contents: Scanning Tunneling Microscopy on High Temperature Superconductors at Low Temperatures (H. Sugawara, M. Nantoh, T. Hasegawa and K. Kitazawa); Scanning Tunneling Microscopy and Josephson Tunneling of High Tc YBCO Oxide Thin Films (H.C. Yang, L. M. Wang, J.H. Lu and H.W. Yu); Investigation of HTS Surface Properties

by Tunneling Spectroscopy (A. Plecenik, M. Grajcar, P. Seidel and S. Benacka); Problems in Tunneling Spectroscopy for High Tc Superconductors (R. Aoki and H.M. Murakami); Tunneling Measurements on the Bi-Cuprates and BKBO Bismuthates in Magnetic Fields (P. Samuely); Symmetry of Order Parameters of High Tc Superconductors (Neeraj Khare); Materials and Device Engineering in High Temperature Superconductor Josephson Junctions and Squids (Q.X. Jia, X.D. Wu and D.W. Reagor); Subject Index.

[D]United States. Congress. House. Committee on the
Budget. Task Force on Defense, Foreign Policy, and Space.
Establishing priorities in science funding :
hearing before the Task Force on Defense, Foreign Policy, and
Space of the Committee on the Budget, House of
Representatives, One Hundred Second Congress, first session,
July 11 and 18, 1991.
Washington : G.P.O. : For sale by the U.S.
G.P.O., Supt. of Docs., Congressional Sales Office, 1991.
KF27.B8439 1991

[D]United States. Congress. House. Committee on
Energy and Commerce. Subcommittee on Oversight and
Investigations.
Mismanagement of DOE's Super Collider : hearing
before the Subcommittee on Oversight and Investigations of
the Committee on Energy and Commerce, House of
Representatives, One Hundred Third Congress, first session,
June 30, 1993.
Washington : U.S. G.P.O. : For sale by the U.S.
G.P.O., Supt. of Docs., Congressional Sales Office, 1994.
KF27.E5546 1993i

[D]United States. Congress. House. Committee on
Science and Technology. Subcommittee on Energy Development
and Applications.
Status and plans of the United States and CERN
high energy physics programs and the Superconducting Super
Collider (SSC) : hearing before the Subcommittee on Energy
Development and Applications of the Committee on Science and
Technology, House of Representatives, Ninety-ninth Congress,
first session, October 29, 1985.
Washington : U.S. G.P.O., 1986.
KF27.S3934 1985e

[D]United States. Congress. House. Committee on
Science, Space, and Technology. Subcommittee on Energy
Research and Development.
Superconductivity : hearing before the

Subcommittee on Energy Research and Development of the Committee on Science, Space, and Technology, House of Representatives, One Hundredth Congress, first session, October 20, 1987.
Washington : U.S. G.P.O. : For sale by the Supt. of Docs., Congressional Sales Office, U.S. G.P.O., 1988.
KF27.S3935 1987e

[D]United States. Congress. House. Committee on Science, Space, and Technology. Subcommittee on Transportation, Aviation, and Materials.
Superconductivity : hearing before the Subcommittee on Transportation, Aviation, and Materials and the Subcommittee on Science, Research, and Technology of the Committee on Science, Space, and Technology, House of Representatives, One Hundredth Congress, first session, October 7, 1987.
Washington : U.S. G.P.O. : For sale by the Supt. of Docs., Congressional Sales Office, U.S. G.P.O., 1988.
KF27.S3997 1987k

[D]United States. Congress. House. Committee on Science, Space, and Technology.
Superconductivity : hearing before the Committee on Science, Space, and Technology, House of Representatives, One hundredth Congress, first session, June 10, 1987.
Washington : U.S. G.P.O. : For sale by Supt. of Docs., Congressional Sales Office, U.S. G.P.O., 1988.
KF27.S39 1987f

[D]United States. Congress. House. Committee on Science, Space, and Technology. Subcommittee on Energy Research and Development.
High-temperature superconductivity technology transfer : hearing before the Subcommittee on Energy Research and Development of the Committee on Science, Space, and Technology, House of Representatives, One Hundredth Congress, second session, June 23, 1988.
Washington : U.S. G.P.O. : For sale by the Supt. of Docs., Congressional Sales Office, U.S. G.P.O., 1988.
KF27.S3935 1988

[D]United States. Congress. House. Committee on
Science, Space, and Technology. Subcommittee on International
Scientific Cooperation.
International cooperation on the Superconducting
Super Collider (SSC) : hearing before the Subcommittee on
International Scientific Cooperation of the Committee on
Science, Space, and Technology, U.S. House of
Representatives, One hundredth Congress, first session, May 7, 1987.
Washington : U.S. G.P.O. : For sale by the Supt.
of Docs., Congressional Sales Office, U.S. G.P.O., 1987.
KF27.S3973 1987a

[D]United States. Congress. House. Committee on
Science, Space, and Technology.
Superconducting super collider : hearings before
the Committee on Science, Space, and Technology, House of
Representatives, One Hundredth Congress, first session, April
7, 8, 9, 1987.
Washington : U.S. G.P.O. : For sale by the Supt.
of Docs., Congressional Sales Office, U.S. G.P.O., 1988.
KF27.S39 1987g

[D]United States. Congress. House. Committee on
Science, Space, and Technology. Subcommittee on International
Scientific Cooperation.
International participation in the
Superconducting Super Collider (SSC) : hearing before the
Subcommittee on International Scientific Cooperation of the
Committee on Science, Space, and Technology, U.S. House of
Representatives, One Hundredth Congress, second session,
March 16, 1988.
Washington : U.S. G.P.O. : For sale by the Supt.
of Docs., Congressional Sales Office, 1988.
KF27.S3973 1988

[D]United States. Congress. House. Committee on
Science, Space, and Technology.
Superconducting Super Collider : hearing before
the Committee on Science, Space, and Technology, U.S. House
of Representatives, One Hundredth Congress, second session,
March 22, 1988.
Washington : U.S. G.P.O. : For sale by the Supt.
of Docs., Congressional Sales Office, U.S. G.P.O., 1989.
KF27.S39 1988b

[D]United States. Congress. House. Committee on
Science, Space, and Technology. Subcommittee on International
Scientific Cooperation.

Superconducting Super Collider project : hearing before the Subcommittee on International Scientific Cooperation of the Committee on Science, Space, and Technology, U.S. House of Representatives, One Hundred First Congress, first session, March 8, 1989.
Washington : U.S. G.P.O. : For sale by the Supt. of Docs., Congressional Sales Office, U.S. G.P.O., 1989.
KF27.S3973 1989

[D]United States. Congress. House. Committee on Science, Space, and Technology.
Review of the site selection process for the Superconducting Super Collider : hearing before the Committee on Science, Space, and Technology, U.S. House of Representatives, One Hundred First Congress, first session, April 5, 1989.
Washington : U.S. G.P.O. : For sale by the Supt. of Docs., Congressional Sales Office, U.S. G.P.O., 1989.
KF27.S39 1989d

[D]United States. Congress. House. Committee on Science, Space, and Technology. Subcommittee on Investigations and Oversight.
Status of the Superconducting Super Collider Program : hearing before the Subcommittee on Investigations and Oversight of the Committee on Science, Space, and Technology, U.S. House of Representatives, One Hundred Second Congress, first session, May 9, 1991.
Washington : U.S. G.P.O. : For sale by the U.S. G.P.O., Supt. of Docs., Congressional Sales Office, 1991.
KF27.S3975 1991b

[D]United States. Congress. House. Committee on Science, Space, and Technology.
The Superconducting Super Collider Project : hearing before the Committee on Science, Space, and Technology, U.S. House of Representatives, One Hundred Third Congress, first session, May 26, 1993.
Washington : U.S. G.P.O. : For sale by the U.S. G.P.O., Supt. of Docs., Congressional Sales Office, 1993.
KF27.S39 1993h

[D]United States. Congress. House. Committee on Science, Space, and Technology. Subcommittee on Investigations and Oversight.
The status of the Superconducting Super Collider : hearing before the Subcommittee on Investigations and Oversight of the Committee on Science, Space, and Technology,

U.S. House of Representatives, One Hundred Second Congress, second session, April 9, 1992.
Washington : U.S. G.P.O. : For sale by the U.S. G.P.O., Supt. of Docs., Congressional Sales Office, 1993.
KF27.S3975 1992h

[D]United States. Congress. House. Committee on Science, Space, and Technology. Subcommittee on Science.
Termination of the Superconducting Super Collider Project : hearing before the Subcommittee on Science of the Committee on Science, Space, and Technology, U.S. House of Representatives, One Hundred Third Congress, second session, March 15, 1994.
Washington : U.S. G.P.O. : For sale by the U.S. G.P.O., Supt. of Docs., Congressional Sales Office, 1994.
KF27.S399 1994a

[D]United States. Congress. Senate. Committee on Energy and Natural Resources. Subcommittee on Energy Research and Development.
Superconducting Super Collider : hearing before the Subcommittee on Energy Research and Development of the Committee on Energy and Natural Resources, United States Senate, One Hundredth Congress, first session on the Department of Energy's funding request for the superconducting super collider, April 7, 1987.
Washington : U.S. G.P.O : For sale by the Supt. of Docs., Congressional Sales Office, U.S. G.P.O., 1988.
KF26.E554 1987d

[D]United States. Congress. Senate. Committee on Energy and Natural Resources. Subcommittee on Energy Research and Development.
Basic science budget and SSC : hearing before the Subcommitte on Energy Research and Development of the Committee on Energy and Natural Resources, United States Senate, One Hundredth Congress, second session on the Department of Energy's fiscal year 1989 request for the superconducting super collider and the basic science budget, April 12, 1988.
Washington : U.S. G.P.O. : For sale by the Supt. of Docs., Congressional Sales Office, U.S. G.P.O., 1988.
KF26.E554 1988b

[D]United States. Congress. Senate. Committee on Energy and Natural Resources. Subcommittee on Energy Research and Development.
Superconducting Super Collider program and the

Department of Energy's budget for fundamental science :
hearing before the Subcommittee on Energy Research and
Development of the Committee on Energy and Natural Resources,
United States Senate, One Hundred First Congress, second
session, ... April 24, 1990.
Washington : U.S. G.P.O. : For sale by the Supt.
of Docs., Congressional Sales Office, U.S. G.P.O., 1990.
KF26.E554 1990

[D]United States. Congress. Senate. Committee on
Energy and Natural Resources. Subcommittee on Energy Research
and Development.
Department of Energy's Superconducting Super
Collider project : hearing before the Subcommittee on Energy
Research and Development of the Committee on Energy and
Natural Resources, United States Senate, One Hundred Second
Congress, first session ... April 16, 1991.
Washington : U.S. G.P.O. : For sale by the Supt.
of Docs., Congressional Sales Office, U.S. G.P.O., 1991.
KF26.E554 1991

[D]United States. Congress. Senate. Committee on
Energy and Natural Resources.
Importance and status of the Superconducting
Super Collider : joint hearing before the Committee on Energy
and Natural Resources and the Subcommittee on Energy and
Water Development of the Committee on Appropriations, United
States Senate, One Hundred Second Congress, second session
... June 30, 1992.
Washington : U.S. G.P.O. : For sale by the U.S.
G.P.O., Supt. of Docs., Congressional Sales Office, 1992.
KF26.E55 1992q

[D]United States. Congress. Senate. Committee on
Energy and Natural Resources.
Superconducting Super Collider : joint hearing
before the Committee on Energy and Natural Resources and the
Subcommittee on Energy and Water Development of the Committee
on Appropriations, United States Senate, One Hundred Third
Congress, first session, on the Department of Energy's
Superconducting Super Collider project, August 4, 1993.
Washington : U.S. G.P.O. : For sale by the U.S.
G.P.O., Supt. of Docs., Congressional Sales Office, 1993.
KF26.E55 1993g

[D]University of Birmingham Superconductivity
http://www.cm.ph.bham.ac.uk/Useful_Superconductivity_Links.html
Interesting Links to Superconductivity Related Web Sites

Institute of Physics Superconductivity Group UK Superconductivity Forum IRC in Superconductivity, University of Cambridge: $HoNi_2B_2C$ Local Hall Probe Array Studies University of Maryland's Research Group: Magnetic Flux Lattice using Small Angle Neutron Scattering (SANS) Superconductivity and Magnetism Group, Argonne National Laboratory Applied Superconductivity Center, The University of Wisconsin-Madison: Superconductor Image Gallery Magneto-Optical Imaging Magnetically levitated trains, Railway Technical Research Institute (RTRI), Tokyo, Japan Chemistry of the Solid-State, The McDevitt Research Group, University of Texas at Austin Observation of Dynamic Interaction of Vortices with Pinning Centers by Lorentz Microscopy, American Association for the Advancement of Science

[D]University of Wisconsin Applied Superconductivity Center
Address: http://www.engr.wisc.edu/centers/asc/links.html
Includes the following links to centers of applied superconductity. Argonne National Laboratory -- Superconductivity Program Brookhaven National Laboratory Fermi National Accelerator Laboratory Lawrence Livermore National Laboratory Oak Ridge National Laboratory -- Superconductivity ProgramNational High Magnetic Field Laboratory Stanford Linear Accelerator Center Very Large Hadron ColliderCenter for Superconducting Digital ElectronicsCenter for Superconductivity Research Science and Technology Center for Superconductivity The Texas Center for Superconductivity CERNSUPRASPohang Superconductivity Center Railway Technical Research Institute

[D]Utah Cedar Mountains SSC site : U.S.G.S. 7 1/2
minute quadrangle maps showing : A. proposed locations of SSC
facilities : B. Geologic maps along SSC tunnel alignment.
[S.l. : s.n.], 1987.
G1517.C46N35U8 1987

[D]Visocky, A. P. (Adrian P.)
Ground-water investigations for siting the
Superconducting Super Collider in northeastern Illinois / by
Adrian P. Visocky and Marcia K. Schulmeister.
Champaign (2204 Griffith Dr., Champaign 61820) :
Illinois State Water Survey, 1988.
GB705.I3A25 no. 170; Alternative class.:
TD224.I3

[D]Vleeming, Bertus Johan, 1971-
The four-terminal SQUID / Bertus Johan Vleeming.
[Leiden : University of Leiden, 1998]
TK7872.S8V54 1998

[D]Vvedenskiæi, V. L. (Viktor L'vovich)
Sverkhchuvstvitel'naëiìa magnitometriëiìa i
biomagnetizm / V.L. Vvedenskiæi, V.I. Ozhogin.
Moskva : "Nauka," Glav. red.
fiziko-matematicheskoæi lit-ry, 1986.

TK7872.S8V84 1986

[D]Watkins, Chris; Drilling for gravity; New Scientist.v. 156 Oct. 11 '97 p. 6.
A new robust and accurate instrument should make drilling for oil more reliable. A gradiometer constructed around a superconducting string of atoms maintained at supercool by liquid helium has been developed. The miniature deformations created by changes in the gravitational gradient along the string are detected by a superconducting quantum interference device. This sensor has the ability to separate changes in gravity from perturbations generated by acceleration.

[D]Webre, Philip.
Risks and benefits of building the
Superconducting Super Collider.
Washington, D.C. : Congress of the U.S.,
Congressional Budget Office : For sale by the Supt. of Docs.,
U.S. G.P.O., [1988]
QC787.P7W43 1988

[D]Weinstock, Harold and Richard W. Ralston
The New superconducting electronics / edited by
Harold Weinstock and Richard W. Ralston.
Dordrecht ; Boston : Kluwer Academic Publishers, 1993.
TK7872.S8N38 1993

[D]Williams, John Eric Charles.
Superconductivity and its applications [by] J. E. C. Williams.
London, Pion, 1970.
QC612.S8W5

[D]Wilson, Martin N.
Superconducting magnets / Martin N. Wilson.
Oxford [Oxfordshire]: Clarendon Press ; New York
: Oxford University Press, 1983.
QC761.3.W54 1983

[D]Wilson, William F.
Superconducting super collider : location,
geology, and road log / by William F. Wilson and P. Albert
Carpenter III.
[Raleigh, NC]: N.C. Geological Survey, Division
of Land Resources, Department of Environment, Health and
Natural Resources, 1997.
QC787.P7W55 1997

[D]Wisconsin Superconductive Energy Storage Project.
Madison, Wis. : Engineering Experiment Station,
College of Engineering, University of Wisconsin, [1974]-<1983
TK2985.W57 1974

[D]Wolsky, A.M., et al.
Applied superconductivity
[et al.] in collaboration with R.A. Thomas ... [et al.] ;
Department of Defense.
Park Ridge, N.J., U.S.A. : Noyes Data Corp., c1989.
TK7872.S8A67 1989

[D]Wood, Robert W.,
Understanding magnetism : magnets,
electromagnets, and superconducting magnets / Robert W. Wood.
Blue Ridge Summit, PA : Tab Books, 1988.
QC753.5.W66 1988

[D]Workshop on Physics at Future Accelerators (1987
La Thuile, Italy and Geneva, Switzerland)
Proceedings of the Workshop on Physics at Future
Accelerators, La Thuile (Italy) and Geneva (Switzerland),
7-13 January 1987.
Geneva : European Organization for Nuclear
Research, 1987.
QC770.E82 1987 no. 7; Alternative class.:
QC787.P73

[D]Yamamoto, Akira and Tetsuya Yoshida
Workshop on Balloon-Borne Experiment With a
Superconducting Magnet Spectrometer (6th : 1996 : KEK)
Proceedings of the 6th Workshop on Balloon-Borne
Experiment with a Superconducting Magnet Spectrometer : held
at National Laboratory for High Energy Physics (KEK), Jan.,
29-31, 1996 / edited by Akira Yamamoto and Tetsuya Yoshida.
Oho, Tsukuba-shi, Ibaraki-ken, Japan : Natinal
Laboratory for High Energy Physics, 1996.
QC793.5.P727W67 1996

[D]Yamamoto, Akira
Workshop on Balloon-Borne Experiment With a
Superconducting Magnet Spectrometer (5th : 1994 : KEK)
Proceedings of the 5th Workshop on Balloon-Borne
Experiment With a Superconducting Magnet Spectrometer : held
at National Laboratory for High Energy Physics (KEK), Nov. 30
- Dec. 1, 1994 / edited by Akira Yamamoto.
Oho, Tsukuba-shi, Ibaraki-ken, Japan : National
Laboratory for High Energy Physics, 1995.
QC787.S6W67 1994

[D]Yan, Yiton T., James P. Naples, Michael J. Syphers
Accelerator physics at the superconducting super
collider / Yiton T. Yan, James P. Naples, Michael J. Syphers, editors.

Woodbury, NY : American Institute of Physics,
1995.

[D]Yeshurun, Yosef.
Agirat energyah bi-selilim molikhe-°al
be-òtemperaòturot gevohot : duaòh shenati, 1995 / Yosef Yeshurun.
Medinat Yiâsra'el : Miâsrad ha-energyah
òveha-tashtit, Agaf meòhòkar u-fituaòh, [1996]
TK2985.Y47 1996

[D]Z.L. Miropolsky, R.I.Soziev
Gidrodinamika i teploobmen v sverkhprovodnikovykh
ustroæistvakh. English.
Fluid dynamics and heat transfer in
superconducting equipment / [edited by]Z.L. Miropolsky, R.I. Soziev.
New York : Hemisphere Pub., c1990.
TK7871.85.G4513 1989

[D]Zhou, Shu-Ang.
Electrodynamics of solids and microwave
superconductivity / Shu-Ang Zhou.
New York : John Wiley, 1999.
QC631.Z565 1999

Author Index

D

E

F

G

H

I

J

K

L

M

T

U

V

Subject Index

H

I

J

K

L

M